ePublish

Self-Publish Fast and Profitably
for Kindle, iPhone, CreateSpace
and Print on Demand

By Steve Weber
All Rights Reserved © 2009 by Stephen W. Weber

No part of this book may be reproduced or transmitted in any form by any means, graphic, electronic, or mechanical, including photocopying, recording, taping or by any information storage or retrieval system, without permission in writing from the publisher.

Warning and Disclaimer: The information in this book is offered with the understanding that it does not contain legal, financial, or other professional advice. Individuals requiring such services should consult a competent professional.

The author and publisher make no representations about the suitability of the information contained in this book for any purpose. This material is provided "as is" without warranty of any kind.

Although every effort has been made to ensure the accuracy of the contents of this book, errors and omissions can occur. The publisher assumes no responsibility for any damages arising from the use of this book, or alleged to have resulted in connection with this book. This book is not completely comprehensive. Some readers may wish to consult additional books for advice. This book is not authorized or endorsed by Amazon or any other company mentioned in the text.

Published by Stephen W. Weber
Printed in the United States of America
Weber Books   www.WeberBooks.com

Author: Steve Weber
Editor: Julie Bird

ISBN: 978-0-9772406-5-4

Also by Steve Weber:

Plug Your Book! Online Book Marketing for Authors

Sell on Amazon: A Guide to Amazon's Marketplace, Seller Central, and Fulfillment by Amazon Programs

The Home-Based Bookstore: Start Your Own Business Selling Used Books

eBay 101: Selling on eBay For Part-time or Full-time Income

Contents

WAG THE LONG TAIL 57

RISE ABOVE THE NOISE 71

GRADUATE TO PRINT 81

WRITE OFF YOUR EXPENSES 93

MORE RESOURCES 103

INDEX 107

Introduction

The book world is coming unglued.

After years of consolidating, the big publishers are bigger than ever. But readers are buying less. So the Goliaths are downsizing, retrenching, and deflating. Houghton Mifflin recently quit buying manuscripts, like a bakery giving up on making dough.

If you're a new writer, it's harder than ever to get a book contract—unless, of course, you're already famous. If you're not Hillary Clinton, Paris Hilton, or on the FBI's most-wanted list, you probably won't even get an advance.

Book prices are up, and bookstores are dropping like flies. Just two big chains survive, with Barnes & Noble shutting unprofitable stores, and Borders teetering at bankruptcy. Independents are little more than a memory—since 1990, more than half have gone bust.

Authors who do find a publisher discover it's harder to get attention. More than 250,000 new titles are released every year, double the capacity of a book superstore. More than ever, readers are shopping at Amazon.com, which just supplanted Barnes & Noble as the world's largest book retailer. Wikipedia, the free online encyclopedia, has helped kill off World Book, Britannica, and Compton's.

Is the book dead? No, it's just changing. The old world of typesetting, printing, shipping, wholesaling, warehousing, distributing and retailing books is giving way to ePublishing. Now every author can be his or her own publisher, with global reach. Your own brand, your own paycheck.

Technology has made it much easier for aspiring authors to publish without hefty upfront costs. Gone are the days when self-publishing meant paying a printer to produce hundreds of copies that then languished in a garage.

— The New York Times, Jan. 28, 2009

For the first time in history, authors aren't dependent on a publishing food chain. Self-publishing, until recently a last resort, has suddenly become the smart option for authors who want more control and decent money. Everyone wins except the old gatekeepers. Authors can write more and earn more, while readers can read more and pay less.

Today is the Golden Age of publishing. There has never been more opportunity to create and distribute your ideas, with virtually no up-front costs for printing, distribution, or marketing.

If you have a book idea, get going. It will change your life. I know. Today I earn five times what I earned when I wrote for hire at a publishing firm. Last year, after expenses, I earned $100,000 on the books I began writing a few years ago. How much would I have earned if I had sold to a "real" publisher? I don't know, but I probably wouldn't be bragging.

In the old days, authors were happy to get an advance of 10 percent of a publisher's receipts. So if a first printing of 5,000 copies of a $15 book sold out, grossing $75,000, the author earned $7,500. If you're a slow writer like I am, that's not even minimum wage!

Compare that with a book I published last year, *eBay 101*. The book sold 3,192 paperback copies during the year at $15.16 wholesale, a drop in the bucket for a big publisher. For me, it was a big deal: a profit of $34,734. That's $10.90 per book, a royalty rate of *71 percent*.

It might be worth selling your manuscript to a big publisher if that guaranteed a bigger paycheck, but it doesn't.

Perhaps a big publisher could have sold a few more copies of my eBay book. On the other hand, if it had been treated like most mass-produced books, the bookstore chains would have slashed its price after a few months, then returned most copies to the publisher. The remains would have been sold for pennies on the dollar or ground into pulp, and that would have been the end of it.

But I'm still publishing my eBay book. In fact, *eBay 101* is selling even better this year. Because it's printed on-demand, only after copies are sold, I can update it any time. I don't invest a dime in printing, warehousing or shipping.

Because I didn't sell my digital rights to a publisher, I also have an eBook edition, generating more income. Last week, the world's biggest audiobook distributor asked if I would sell the rights to record *eBay 101* as an audiobook. Frankly, I hadn't thought of it—but I just might.

Then again, I might do it myself.

Communities trump companies

This book isn't just about self-publishing. It's about a new way of writing and connecting with readers. ePublishing begins with digital composition, using the word processor and other tools you probably already use. Everything else you need will be explained here:

- How to publish your work digitally for Internet and mobile readers.
- Getting feedback to improve your writing.
- Expanding into paper books, using no-inventory digital printing.

No longer must new writers "pay their dues" by working for free and getting rejection notes. Now you can upload your sample chapter or short story to Amazon and other platforms and, within minutes, start selling it.

Now, a disclaimer: I'm not saying *everyone* should publish. Frankly, I don't know if you can write or not, and that's the hard part. The stuff in this book is easy.

> *A writer is someone for whom writing is more difficult than it is for other people.*

> **— Thomas Mann**

But let's assume you've got the talent. You still need help. A decent book requires an experienced editor, a cover designer, and some advice now and then. I'll explain where you can get this help.

This book isn't about shortcuts or getting rich without working. If you aren't the type of writer who has the focus to revise your work 20 times, 30 times, or 50 times, then self-publishing isn't for you. And you won't find any writing advice here, except this:

- Write what you know
- Get feedback
- Revise, revise, revise

Working three months, six months or a year to finish a book is a steep climb when the payoff is distant and uncertain. Just start. The thing that will keep you going is *reader feedback*. Every time you finish a section, you can sell the installment online, or give it away free. Instead of facing the impossible task of writing a book all at once, break it up. You can get paid for each installment, and more importantly, get reader feedback, which can guide and motivate you.

Then, you can publish a "beta" edition of your book, and get more reader feedback. You'll tweak your book some more, then digitally print a paperback. I'll show you how to get the reviews and sales momentum to make your book a success.

But what if I don't need to self-publish?

What if your book has blockbuster potential, and you don't want to blow your chance at immortality and a fat check from Random House? Some warn that self-publishing makes your "first publishing rights" less valuable to a big publisher.

Maybe. On the other hand, self-publishing can make your rights *more valuable* to the right publisher. Just like Hollywood, most publishers love a proven idea with a built-in audience. Take this advice from Julia Fox Garrison, who self-published her memoir before selling it to Harper-Collins:

> *I advise all would-be authors to self-publish. Having a finished product allows you to maintain control and*

leverage. ... A book's success is directly related to the extent to which it is marketed, regardless of pedigree.

— Time Magazine, February 2009

In reality, the notion that big publishers don't buy self-published books is bunk. Simon & Schuster paid $4.2 million for Rick Evans' 87-page story *The Christmas Box*. Warner Books paid James Redfield $800,000 for *The Celestine Prophecy* after he sold 100,000 copies himself. After 17-year-old Christopher Paolini self-pubbed *Eragon*, he sold it and scored a blockbuster book and a film grossing $249 million.

Yes, the conventional wisdom is to shop a mass-market manuscript to agents and publishers first. But why wait six months, a year, or two years just to hear "No"? Or, more likely, no answer at all?

Just say "Yes." Then do it.

STEVE WEBER
feedback@WeberBooks.com

Dive into electronic text

What, exactly, is an eBook? It's a book in an electronic, digital format without paper. If you haven't explored eBooks yet, take a look at Feedbooks:

www.feedbooks.com

Here you can browse thousands of free eBooks, nicely formatted for whatever kind of gadget you're using. You can download the books to your computer, Internet phone, or eBook reader. If you want, you can print these books, copy or forward them—they're all free, and you don't have to buy anything special. You can view the books online, print them, or import them to your cellphone or dedicated eBook reader.

Although some "pirate" eBook sites distribute illegally copied books, Feedbooks isn't one of them. Its catalog consists mostly of older, public domain content published before 1923, so permission from those publishers isn't required. Some current authors upload their books on Feedbooks, too. To browse these self-published works, click "Share" on the top navigation bar.)

Here's another popular eBook site:

http://manybooks.net/

These sites are increasingly popular because they provide good content in free, easy-to-use formats. A forerunner of these sites is Project Gutenberg at Gutenburg.org.

Most people who read eBooks use a computer—a PC, Mac, or laptop. A smaller but growing group use cellphones and dedicated readers like Amazon's Kindle and the Sony Reader.

eBooks are the fastest-growing part of publishing, with sales increasing about 50 percent annually for the past five years. The world is moving to digital content as costs for electronic storage and delivery fall, while the costs of printing and shipping rise.

Selling points of eBooks are several: They offer instant gratification, need no shelf space, and are seldom lost, damaged, or stolen. Publishers can produce eBooks quickly, in response to news, trends, even fads. With easy revisions, eBooks never go obsolete.

eBooks also fit with today's online shoppers. These shoppers demand value, detailed product information, independent reviews, and easy comparisons. Readers who have embraced eBooks are key members of your audience because they're opinion leaders and early adopters, the people who generate word of mouth.

For years, big publishers have resisted eBooks, fearful they would cannibalize sales of paper books, or pBooks. In fact, just the opposite often happens: Readers who enjoy an eBook often buy the paperback or hardcover, too, and search for more titles by the same author.

Amazon's Kindle is perhaps the most well-known dedicated eBook reader device, simply because of Amazon's fame as a book retailer. The Kindle debuted in 2007 at $399, then was reduced to $359. The Kindle is portable and wireless, downloading books seamlessly through a free cellular service from Amazon. The gadget and the eBooks are sold in Amazon's Kindle Store:

www.kindle.amazon.com

Kindle users can also read free texts from sites such as Feedbooks, although it's not as easy as buying from Amazon. The files must be e-mailed and converted, or the Kindle connected to a computer with a USB cable.

Users of Apple's iPhone can purchase Kindle editions too, which has significantly expanded the market for eBooks.

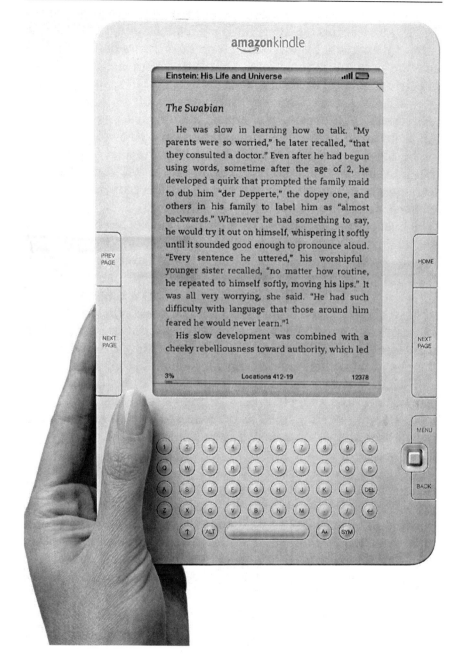

Amazon's Kindle eBook reader is about the size of a thin paperback book, a third of an inch thick. It uses a cellphone network to download books from Amazon. "Our vision is 'every book ever printed, in every language, all available in 60 seconds,'" says Jeff Bezos, Amazon chief executive.

The Kindle has two big attractions for readers: a bigger catalog of current books, and big discounts. *New York Times* bestsellers cost only $9.99 in the Kindle Store, while hardcovers are $16 or more. The first chapter of all Kindle books is free.

Kindle is more than a portable screen. Users can annotate their books, add bookmarks, notes, and highlighting, and all of this is archived at Amazon. If a Kindle is lost or broken, the customer buys a new one, and downloads the books again at no charge. While a Kindle book is displayed, readers can search for synonyms or definitions using the built-in dictionary, and the gadget plays audio files too.

Even more revolutionary than the Kindle hardware is the accompanying Web site for authors. The Digital Text Platform enables anyone to self-publish directly to the Kindle Store and collect royalties of 35 percent.

Many books in the Kindle Store are simply a digital version of existing pBooks. But a Kindle book can be practically anything—a short article, an anthology, or a college dissertation. A publisher might decide to sell the text of a pBook for $9.99 in the Kindle Store, while also charging 99 cents for individual chapters.

Kindle's closest competitor is the Sony Reader, introduced a year earlier. Both gadgets use an "E-ink" screen that mimics real paper and ink, avoiding the eyestrain caused by computer screens. Many lesser-known eReader-type products are on the market or in the works.

Despite the sizzle of Kindle and its competitors, the device used most often for mobile reading is the familiar cellphone. Most noteworthy is the Apple iPhone, because of its explosive sales growth and easy access to paid content, including Kindle books. Millions of readers already own an iPhone, primarily for other uses—as a phone, camera, e-mail device, or game machine.

Few people buy a cellphone intending to read books on it, but many end up doing just that, perhaps while sitting in traffic or standing in line. The iPhone's screen is smaller and its battery life is shorter than Kindle's, but there are 20 million in use, with a million more sold every month. By contrast, Amazon has sold only 500,000 to 750,000 Kindles (a guess, because Amazon doesn't disclose sales figures).

The Sony eBook Reader.

Indeed, a variety of publishers, including O'Reilly Media Inc., report that book sales in the iPhone's "application store" are brisker than sales of the same titles in the Kindle Store. In fact, one of O'Reilly's iPhone eBooks outsold the pBook version—even while that paperback was the top-selling computer book in the world.

Open your book; open your mind

Some traditionalists complain that eBooks are a pale imitation of pBooks. True, old-fashioned books are a great technology—portable, reusable, and no batteries required. But let's consider what is *gained* with ePublishing.

eBooks can include multimedia files—audio and video. ePublishing is still in its infancy, with most books just becoming available in digital formats. The big change will come when multiple books and readers are linked, annotated, and analyzed. Then, when you see something mentioned in a footnote, you'll be able to jump to that referenced item, just like when you're surfing the

Web. You can ask the author a question, leave a comment, or join a book club discussing the book.

Let's take a look at how one new author, Scott Sigler, embraced ePublishing and became a rising star. After years of writing, Sigler had nothing to show for it except a stack of rejection slips. Then Sigler heard about "podcasting," a kind of Internet radio. He started recording episodes from his book, *EarthCore*, using a microphone plugged into his computer. He recorded the episodes in his apartment's walk-in closet, standing between the hanging shirts to muffle street noise.

Word spread, and every week thousands more listeners downloaded the free episodes to their computer, iPod, or portable music player. By the time he was finished, Sigler had 30,000 listeners, a literary agent, and a hardcover bestseller.

Since then Sigler has scored two more bestselling books, and Random House is selling audiobook versions for $34.95. Nobody seems to mind that anyone can already listen to, read, or print the stories from Sigler's Web site. In fact, the exposure just brings more fans to Sigler, fueling more word of mouth, more sales.

Despite its relatively small size and short battery life, the multifunction iPhone is used to read eBooks more often than any other portable device.

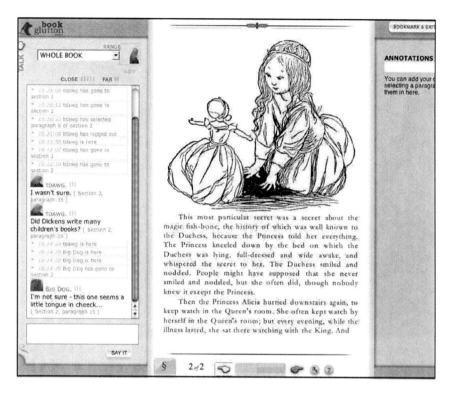

A glimpse of the past and future of books: *Alice in Wonderland* as seen on an online social network, BookGlutton.com. Panels on each side allow readers to annotate and discuss the book, publicly or privately. Users can filter chats by chapter or entire book. Members can publish their own books to the site.

Nonfiction authors have succeeded with podcasting, too, perhaps none better than Mignon Fogarty, host of *Grammar Girl*. She got the idea for a show about grammar tips because, from years of editing, she had lots of advice to give. She made a new podcast every week, although sometimes the recording was interrupted when her upstairs neighbors started doing the laundry.

Fogarty's five-minute grammar lessons were a nice blend of useful advice and entertainment. Her weekly audience quickly swelled to 100,000. Suddenly, she got a book contract from Holt and was invited to appear on *The Oprah Winfrey Show*. Because the show aired before she finished writing, Fogarty cobbled together an audiobook using existing material she planned for the book.

Mignon Fogarty was an unknown editor and science writer until she struck gold with her *Grammar Girl* podcast. With a new twist, she got famous the old-fashioned way—by word of mouth.

After her appearance, the audiobook topped the chart on iTunes, the Apple music and audio store. By the time *Grammar Girl's Quick and Dirty Tips for Better Writing* was in paperback, there was a built-in audience, making it a reference bestseller. Steady exposure from the podcast has fueled continued sales.

Networking your book

Traditional books are published into a set form. The author, editor and proofreaders finish, and the die is cast—unless the book was one of the relatively few popular enough to survive for another edition. No wonder they're called "dead-tree" books.

ePublishing allows a book to stay fluid, open to new facts and contributors. These "networked" books are designed to be continually updated. For example, *Gamer Theory* by McKenzie Wark exists as a hardcover, but was originally written on a Web site as the author proceeded, taking suggestions from readers:

www.futureofthebook.org/gamertheory

Gamer Theory is presented as nine chapters of 25 paragraphs each. Visually, it resembles a stack of colored index cards, each containing a paragraph from the author, along with reader comments. Only a few comments were used in the book, but many of them influenced Wark's final draft.

A networked book doesn't require a flashy Web site or a big name. One of the best things you can do for your readers and yourself is to simply print your e-mail address in your book's introduction. Ask for reader comments, suggestions, and corrections. In return, you'll get a gold mine of ideas for new editions, books, and spinoffs.

When books are connected, they come to life. The mere suggestion that you're open to ideas from readers inspires their loyalty. That's something they rarely get from the big guys.

Publish to the Kindle Store

Here's a good place to get your feet wet. Self-publishing your content to the Kindle Store is relatively simple using Amazon's Digital Text Platform. Amazon converts your file to Kindle format and offers it for sale.

If you already have a buying or selling account at Amazon, you can log in with your existing e-mail address and password here:

www.dtp.amazon.com

You'll be asked to agree to the terms and conditions of Amazon's digital books program. To ensure you receive royalties, click the "My Account" tab on the DTP Dashboard, click "Add Or Edit Account," and add your bank account number. You'll also need to provide your full name and a tax identification number so the income can be reported to the Internal Revenue Service.

Amazon pays Kindle authors a royalty of 35 percent of retail, the list price you set for your eBook. For example, let's imagine you list your book at $13.95. For each sale, Amazon pays you 35 percent, or $4.88. Even if Amazon discounts your title and charges buyers only $9.99, you'll still receive your royalty of $4.88 per sale. The funds are wired to the bank account you specify while registering at DTP. You can track your Kindle sales at the DTP tab called "My Reports." Amazon pays about 60 days after the end of the calendar month in which the sales occur.

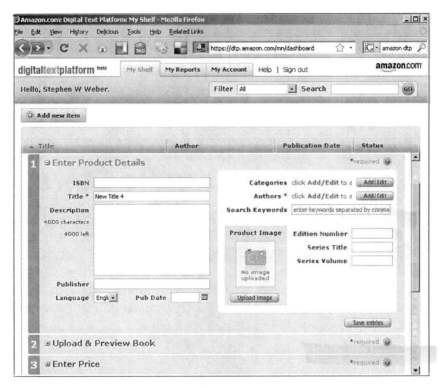

Amazon's Digital Text Platform dashboard enables publishers to upload or post revised content to the Kindle Store. See dtp.amazon.com

Format for the Kindle

Before uploading your writing to Amazon, save the document in HTML format. Most of your formatting, such as bold and italicized letters, should be preserved. Certain things, however, might not translate, such as tables or grids of information. So you may want to replace your tables with some plain text or, if possible, replace this content with images. For more details on Kindle formatting, see the section below on "Resolve Kindle format issues."

Enter details and name your price

From the DTP desktop, click the "My Shelf" tab, then click the "Add New Item" button. A box will open, where you can:

- Enter details about your book.
- Upload your book's text.
- Specify the price.

Each of these three steps is marked with a red X, and as you complete each step, the red X is replaced by a green check mark. The form works well only with plain text—in other words, you shouldn't insert HTML or text copied directly from a Microsoft Word document, or you may accidentally apply some hidden formatting that will show up later on Amazon's Web site.

Next you'll enter the product details. Title and author are the only required fields. But to increase the odds of Amazon shoppers discovering your book when they search for keywords or subjects, you'll want to enter as much descriptive information as possible.

A separate field is provided for each of these details:

- **ISBN.** Amazon doesn't require an ISBN for your Kindle book. When an existing pBook edition of your book is available on Amazon, you should enter its ISBN here. This will help Amazon migrate the customer reviews for your paper edition to your Kindle edition's page.
- **Title.** Enter the title and subtitle. If your eBook is part of a series, enter the series title or volume number here.
- **Description.** This is a brief explanation of your book, much like material that appears on the back cover of a paperback or the inside flap of a hardcover. Be as descriptive as possible within the 4,000-character limit.
- **Publisher.** This can be your real name, a nickname, or your publishing company name.
- **Language.** The default is English.
- **Pub Date.** If the same content has been published previously outside Amazon's DTP, enter its original publication date here. Otherwise Amazon will automatically enter the date when it finishes processing your eBook.
- **Categories.** You can select from up to five predefined categories and subcategories to help shoppers find your book,

such as Business & Economics > Business Communication > Business Ethics. Use as many appropriate categories as you can find to increase the chances that readers will find your eBook.

- **Authors.** At least one author name is required, and you can add the names of other contributors, including editors, translators and illustrators.
- **Search Keywords.** Enter five to seven descriptive keywords that shoppers would likely use to find your eBook. Separate the keywords with commas. Use the precise terms that will help the most people find your content. That's how most Amazon buyers find what to buy—searching with keywords.
- **Edition Number.** If your content is being published for the first time, you may enter 1 or leave the field blank. If your eBook has been updated, indicate the edition number.
- **Series Title.** If your content is one of a series of works, enter the series title.
- **Volume Number.** Series novels and magazines often have a volume number, which you may enter here.
- **Product Image.** Upload your cover image here. A cover image isn't mandatory, but an eye-catching image can boost your sales. If your book has been published previously in paper, use the existing cover art.

Preview your Kindle edition

Click "Upload and Preview Book," and provide the file name of your eBook. Amazon will accept any of five formats: Microsoft Word, HTML, plain text, Adobe PDF, and unencrypted Mobipocket files.

After Amazon's DTP processes your file, click "Preview" to see how it will appear on Amazon's Kindle reader. If you're unsatisfied with the preview, you'll need to download, modify, and upload your content again after fixing the formatting.

After you click "Publish" your eBook should be available for purchase within 24 to 72 hours. After that, it may take a few more days for your book to appear on Amazon with all its descriptive content. If you have a pBook for sale on Amazon, customer reviews should be automatically transferred to your Kindle edition, but this can take a few weeks to process.

Name your price

Enter your list price and click "Save entries." The minimum price is 99 cents, and the maximum price is $200.

If you've completed each step successfully, the progress indicators at the top of the form should show green check marks, and the "Publish" button will be active. Click "Publish" to place your eBook for sale on Amazon.

You can always change the price of your Kindle books after publication, and the change will go into effect almost immediately. You can change your list price and other details for your content later by revisiting the "My Shelf" tab, making the desired changes, clicking "Save entries," and clicking "Publish."

Most readers expect to pay less for eBooks than they pay for pBooks. Most publishers agree that the lower the price, the more units you'll sell. Prices of $10, $15, and $25 are important thresholds.

Many publishers use the same general rules for pricing their eBooks as they've always used for pBooks. They believe that specialized, niche nonfiction work can command a higher price, while shorter entertainment and fiction is expected to be priced lower. Harlequin romance eBooks, for example, cost about $3.50 in the Kindle Store. Unknown, self-published authors often price their work even lower.

It pays to experiment with eBook pricing, then decide what is optimal. But the value of each download can't be calculated in dollars and cents. Some publishers use low-priced or even free eBooks to help build a fan base for new authors, or to promote an author's previous books. The mere availability of an eBook can function like free advertising, which is invaluable.

Free samples, such as excerpts and sample chapters, are worthwhile marketing tools. With the onslaught of new titles released every week, many publishers believe that free content is one of the best ways to get noticed by new readers.

Authors can have other motivations for offering low-cost or free content. Some simply want to spread an idea or story to as many readers as possible, and aren't too concerned about financial rewards. For others, an eBook or pBook might be a lead-generation tool for a different business, such as consulting or professional speaking. Your best pricing strategy depends on what you aim to accomplish with your work.

Some authors wonder whether publishing a Kindle edition at a price lower than an existing pBook will reduce sales of the pBook, but it seems unlikely. Only a small fraction of Amazon customers have bought a Kindle so far. And even when they buy a Kindle, those customers continue buying pBooks at the same rate as before, then also buy double that number of books in Kindle format, according to Jeff Bezos, Amazon's chief executive.

Resolve Kindle formatting issues

If your text is from a book containing references to physical page numbers, you should remove the page numbers before publishing the content to DTP. Remember that Kindle users can resize the text, making your page references incorrect.

If you need further formatting help, check out Kindleformatting.com, an independent service that charges $40 per hour for Kindle formatting. Another alternative is Amazon's BookSurge unit, which converts files to Kindle format for a flat fee of $299.

Even when no special problems occur when uploading your file to Amazon's DTP, there are several ways to optimize your book for Kindle viewing. For example, with some extra effort, you can format hyperlinks within your book, so that page references (or index entries) actually transport the reader to the intended section of the book.

For a step-by-step guide to formatting a Microsoft Word document for Kindle, consult this two free tutorials:

http://www.aprillhamilton.com/resources/HowToUseAmazonDTP_v2.pdf

http://forums.digitaltextplatform.com/dtpforums/entry.jspa?externalID=19&cat-egoryID=7

You can obtain technical support from Amazon employees and other eBook publishers by posting a question to the DTP forum:

http://forums.digitaltextplatform.com/dtpforums

Manage digital rights

Copyright infringement is a prime concern with publishers. pBooks have always been vulnerable to unauthorized photocopy-ing and scanning, but the potential for pirating of digital texts is disconcerting.

Many eBook publishers prevent unauthorized duplication and distribution of their texts by using some form of digital rights management (DRM). In its most restrictive form, DRM might pre-vent the reader from printing the text, copying it, or viewing it on more than one device. At the other end of the spectrum, an "unprotected" eBook might be a simple text file, word-processing document, or anything else that might be freely copied and distrib-uted through the Internet.

Many consumers object to DRM because it interferes with rights they've traditionally enjoyed with physical media. For example, readers of a copy-protected eBook can't loan it to a friend, resell it when finished, or donate it to their library.

The alternative is "open" eBooks without DRM, which would encourage sales with minimal risk of piracy, advocates say. They contend that digital music sales have expanded in the last few years because of the development of one-click purchasing of indi-vidual songs and albums using iPods and other devices. Recently Apple decided to offer non-DRM music in its iTunes Store.

Target the mobile reader

Apple, maker of the ubiquitous iPod music player, wasn't targeting the eBook market when it launched its iPhone smartPhone. "Nobody reads anymore," Apple founder Steve Jobs joked at the time.

Actually, people are reading more than they used to, according to the National Endowment for the Arts. U.S. publishers rake in $16 billion a year, and while it's true that pBook growth has stalled, digital content picks up the slack, especially for publishers who don't botch the job.

iPhone users are always connected to an "App Store" enabling them to buy digital books, audio, video, and shop for thousands of add-on programs. Competition to sell those applications in the App Store has sparked such a gold rush it makes Amazon's Kindle program look like two rusty cans connected with string.

Digital publishers are just one wave of entrepreneurs targeting the iPhone jackpot, along with game makers and providers of travel, sports, productivity, and finance software.

Although its small screen makes it a mediocre tool for long-form reading, some publishers noticed that their sales in the App Store outpaced sales of their same titles on Amazon's Kindle dedicated eBook reader.

Price to sell on the iPhone

As iPhone publishers battled for attention on the original 2007 iPhone, the average price of the bestselling 100 applications plummeted to $4. By the time the second-generation iPhone was launched a year later, the average price was $2.80 and dropping fast.

eBooks aren't immune to this pressure to drop prices, especially those over $10. For example, when O'Reilly Media raised the App Store price of its eBook *iPhone: The Missing Manual* from $4.99 to $9.99, its iPhone sales immediately plummeted by 75 percent.

This reflects a few hard realities of the App Store. What is popular today is often gone by tomorrow. Novelties churn quickly because software makers soon produce knockoffs of the biggest sellers, like recordings of jokes and prank phone calls. Even the "books" category has its share of junk, like hastily formatted files of old public-domain books. It's possible to upload the text of *Dracula* and sell it today for $1, but tomorrow someone new will be there with a new version costing 99 cents.

Commodities are a cutthroat business, but if you publish something new you'll have staying power.

Publishers with unique content have been happy, overall, with sales on the iPhone. When Henry Melton published his first novel, *Emperor Dad*, as an eBook, he didn't know what to expect. He sold practically nothing on the Kindle, so later, he was surprised when the iPhone edition began selling several copies a day. First-mover status probably didn't hurt, either: Melton was one of the first 100 authors on the iPhone.

Comparing App Store and Amazon rankings

Compared with Amazon's data-stuffed Web store, it's a bit harder to gauge the competition on the iPhone. The App Store has a rudimentary sales rank feature, reminiscent of Amazon's Sales Rank feature for books and other categories.

In the App Store rankings, much more weight is given to same-day sales than in Amazon. Perhaps because of the small screen, navigation is more limited in the App Store, but lists of top-selling items are prominent in the App Store. An appearance in the Top 25 can produce a snowball effect, with a flurry of sales.

The iPhone's desktop startup screen, left.

The iPhone App Store, right, where wireless users can purchase and download books and other applications with a single click.

The Top 100 rankings change constantly throughout the day. Rankings are based on the number of downloads. The most frequently downloaded application is ranked No. 1, just as the best-selling book on Amazon is assigned a sales rank of 1. The App Store has separate lists for "paid apps" where the publisher charges a fee, and "free apps" which cost nothing.

Users may review each app they download, from five stars (excellent) to one star (terrible), similar to Amazon's book review feature. The reviews appear on the app's product page. Reviews on the iPhone tend to be less diplomatic than on Amazon. Users who are only mildly disappointed with an app, even a free one, don't hesitate to trash it with a one-star review. Fortunately, it's a level playing field, with plenty of thumbs-down all around.

Besides browsing bestsellers, the main way iPhone users discover a book or application is with keyword searches. If the user searches for the author name or words used in the book's title or App Store product page, then the book appears in search results, ranked by download frequency.

Why would a publisher upload a "free" app to the store? It might be a "trial" or "lite" version containing just some features of a paid version. A free book app might consist of a sample chapter of a paid version.

Like regular eBooks, the App Store can provide big exposure. The more places your book appears, the more it sticks. A certain percentage of the millions of iPhone users browsing the App Store who notice your book but don't buy it today will buy it the next time they're shopping, there or elsewhere.

Go in the App Store's back door

If, like most authors, you're not a computer programmer, you may need assistance with the App Store. This method of publishing requires the book text to be contained in a stand-alone reader program. Fortunately, a growing number of service providers are offering solutions. For example, eBookApp.com can convert your Microsoft Word or text document into an iPhone application. The company charges publishers a fee for converting the file and a percentage of the sales.

Publishing your own books directly to the App Store requires programming expertise, registration as an iPhone developer, and payment of a one-time fee of $99. For more information, see:

http://developer.apple.com/

A different option for publishers without programming skills is a program known as RasterBook. The program converts an HTML book into a set of images, with each image representing a page from the book. The advantage is that you can retain your book's original fonts, colors, illustrations, and other design elements. The disadvantage of RasterBook is that the images require storage space, so books made with the program require more lengthy download time. Also, because the pages are images instead of actual text, your book isn't searchable, and if your text contains hyperlinks, they won't be "clickable" and forward the user to a Web site. For more information:

http://a-i-studio.com/rasterbook/

The disadvantages of RasterBook can be mitigated if you're publishing a "free" application to the App Store, such as sample chapters. To prevent misunderstandings with iPhone users, be sure to add the words "excerpts" or "sample chapters" to your book. Otherwise, you may receive negative reviews from readers who become irritated when they discover they didn't receive the entire book.

If you need a full-service solution to upload your free book to the App Store, TouchBooks Reader will format and upload your book for a flat fee of $491. See:

http://www.touchbooksreader.com/forauthors

An emerging mobile market is phones using the Android software developed by Google and later the Open Handset Alliance. Most of the developers of iPhone eBook tools have plans for Android because it may someday rival the iPhone.

In March 2009, Amazon made its vast catalog of Kindle books available for purchase on the iPhone. Overnight, the free "Kindle for iPhone" application became the most popular eBook reader software for the iPhone. The software allows any Amazon user to view Kindle editions on their iPhone, regardless of whether they own the Kindle hardware. Publishers immediately reported a surge in sales of their Kindle eBooks, with some reporting a quadrupling of daily sales.

Smash your words

Smashwords.com is an innovative service for publishing eBooks. Self-published eBooks are sold on the Web site, and also made available on Kindle, iPhone and elsewhere.

After opening a Smashwords account and uploading your text, your book will be converted into several formats and offered as a download to users of computers and mobile devices like the iPhone and Kindle. The company takes a 15 percent commission on each sale, but if you make your eBook available for free, there is no charge for using Smashwords.

If you publish with Smashwords, you retain all the rights to your work. You can set which formats will be made available and how much of your text can be sampled by users. Smashwords is also a good alternative for publishers without a U.S. bank account.

Smashwords also provides a way for eBook publishers to transition to pBooks. The company has an affiliate relationship with Wordclay.com, enabling users to design a cover, try different book layouts, and specify a royalty rate.

BookLocker.com is a full-service option for eBook authors. The company screens manuscripts, so poor-quality books or those without any commercial appeal are rejected. There is no listing fee for books provided in PDF format. For an additional fee, Book-Locker can also make your book available as a paperback.

Amazon's Mobipocket

Mobipocket, an eBook retailer and wholesaler, is a subsidiary of Amazon.com. It provides free software, the Mobipocket Reader, which allows users of some hand-held computers and cellphones to view eBooks. One noteworthy aspect of Mobipocket is that it provides an alternate way into Amazon's Kindle Store. Titles you upload to Mobipocket will appear in the Kindle Store automatically.

To join Mobipocket, register at its publisher portal, eBook-Base:

www.mobipocket.com/eBookBase/en/homepage/apply.asp?Type=Publisher

To convert your books to the Mobipocket format, you can download a free copy of the necessary software, Mobipocket Creator, Publisher Edition. You'll be able to upload directly from the Mobipocket Creator software using the eBookBase Web interface:

www. Mobipocket.com/eBookBase/en/Homepage/default.asp

When you upload books to Mobipocket, you'll be able to specify which online retailers will be authorized to sell your title. If you select Amazon.com, your book will be made available in Amazon's Kindle format. If your address is in the United States, Amazon will send you an e-mail asking you to provide a U.S. bank account where Amazon can deposit your royalties. Amazon will also ask for a tax identification number, such as your Social Security number or, if your publishing company is incorporated, a federal Tax Identification Number.

If you have already published Kindle books through an Amazon DTP account, you should eliminate "Amazon.com" as an authorized retailer in your Mobipocket account. Otherwise, duplicate listings of your books will appear in the Kindle store.

Mobipocket offers a useful free eBook formatting tool called Mobipocket Creator:

http://www.mobipocket.com/en/downloadSoft/ProductDetailsCreator.asp

Give it away and prosper

Some traditional publishers resist making their content available to digital users. They fear that distributing electronic text might encourage piracy and kill today's cash cow, pBooks. Publishers are understandably cautious—not long ago, the music industry imploded after digital music leaked onto Internet peer-to-peer networks like Napster.

Yet it seems books are different. No evidence supports the idea that publishing or readership are declining because of free content, piracy, or the Web. In fact, free content and even "unauthorized" copies can actually boost sales. The more often your content is copied, quoted, forwarded, or commented upon, the more people who learn of it, buy it, or recommend it to friends.

Consider the experiment Random House conducted with eight new titles last year. The publisher distributed digital copies of the books in 12 formats on various Internet peer-to-peer networks, often used to download unauthorized copies of books, movies, and music. During the six-month experiment, sales of paper editions of those eight titles rose an average of 19 percent. (For more details on the experiment, see *Impact of P2P and Free Distribution on Book Sales*, available through Safari Books Online Rough Cut editions.)

Free trials are a familiar, proven marketing technique in most businesses, so why not publishing?. With digital content, distribution costs virtually nothing. The only question is whether the trial produces enough paying customers or meets some other objective.

Fewer publishers these days fear they'll be "Napsterized" like the music business. Some of them even "pirate" their own content, facilitating peer-to-peer downloads. The biggest P2P search network, Mininova.com, has signed up 1,000 publishers to its two-year-old "content distribution" program. In essence, publishers give away their crown jewels in exchange for top placement in search results.

An easy-to-use alternative to P2P networks is Scribd.com, a social publishing site. Scribd makes it easy to upload and share your writing, and with more than 50 million users, it aims to become the "YouTube" of print. Thanks to an arrangement with Google, authors can get enormous free exposure on Scribd .

Show and sell on Google

Your biggest friend in the information business is the Google search engine because of its universal popularity and influence on Internet traffic. A vast majority of people who buy digital content find what they're looking for by starting at Google.com.

You don't even need a Web site to put Google to work for you. If you allow the search engine to show snippets from your book, Google generates free advertising and sales. Google Book Search, at Books.google.com, allows users to search the full text of enrolled books. Along with your book, Google displays a link to your Web site, and links to retailers selling your book.

Google Book Search can produce a windfall of traffic, enabling many more people to stumble upon your book, even if they weren't exactly looking for it. If a Google.com user searches for words that appear anywhere in your book, a link to your title can appear on Book Search, or even Google's main site, Google.-com.

Safeguards are built into Google Book Search, similar to Amazon's Search Inside the Book. Users can view a limited number of low-resolution page images that can't be printed easily or saved. A portion of the book is kept off-line so users wouldn't be able to see the whole book even if they had several different Google accounts.

The title *Plug Your Book* as shown on Google Book Search

You can profit from Google Book Search even if nobody buys your book. Google runs small advertisements from its AdWords network in the page margins, and splits the ad revenue with publishers. Each time someone clicks on an ad displayed with your book, you get paid a few cents. Some publishers believe this is the future of reference books, that some day all such content will be available free online, subsidized by advertising.

Google's Book Search has signed up 20,000 publishers and its database includes about 7 million books. About 1 million books are shown in "full preview" mode, while another 1 million are in the public domain. The remaining 5 million are out of print, no longer stocked by bookstores. You can get more facts and open a publisher's account here:

http://books.google.com/publishers.html

Book Search has been controversial among some publishers, and prompted a lawsuit from The Authors Guild. But the suit was settled in 2008, paving the way for Google to develop a market-place of digital and printed books. Google is working on a new system to forward payments from book sales, advertising, and library fees to authors and publishers. The initiative includes:

- **Preview.** After searching Google using related keywords, users can preview a certain number of pages of books to help decide whether they want to buy it. (The book rights holder must enroll the book and allow previews through Google's Book Search partner program). Google will display related advertising alongside the book previews and split this revenue with publishers.
- **Consumer Purchase.** Individuals purchase the right to view an entire book online. The rights holder may set the selling price, or allow Google to set the price using an algorithm designed to maximize exposure and revenue. Publishers receive 63 percent of the proceeds and Google keeps 37 percent. When Google displays advertisements alongside book previews, it splits revenue with publishers at this same rate.
- **Institutional Subscriptions.** Corporate, government, and academic institutions can buy full access to books.
- **Free Public Library Access.** At designated computers at U.S. college and public libraries, patrons will have free, full viewing access to books, while revenue will go to publishers when pages are printed.
- **Print on Demand.** In addition to purchasing online access to books, consumers can pay additional fees for printed copies of books.

Google also plans to sell access to older books with expired copyrights.

Enrolling at Google Book Search

To submit your book to Google Book Search, you must own the digital rights. If someone else published your book, check your contract. Also, ensure you meet these criteria:

- You must upload 100 percent of the book's contents (you can set the percentage of pages readers will be able to preview).
- If you supply a link where readers can buy your book, the link must be to your own Web site, not a third-party site. No affiliate links are permitted.
- You can't provide incentives for users to click on the Google advertisements displayed with your book, and you're prohibited from clicking on the ads yourself.

Google has expanded the types of works it accepts for Book Search. Originally, only books with ISBNs were accepted. Later, recognizing that many eBooks and a growing percentage of printed books aren't assigned ISBNs, Google began accepting books without them. However, there is a special procedure for uploading non-ISBN books; you can't add a non-ISBN book directly from your account's "Add Books" page. To submit a non-ISBN book, you must:

- Send a paper copy or upload a PDF file using your Google Book Search account.
- After Google processes the file, the title will appear in your account with a unique identifying code. This could take several days.
- When the title appears in your account, you'll have a chance to modify the settings, such as the "Buy Link," before the title appears in Book Search.

Ready, aim, format!

eBooks come in many flavors, which is a blessing and a curse. Several formats clutter the marketplace because none has become dominant. Although converting your book to various formats is a chore, most recent word-processing programs can save your text as an HTML or PDF file. Also, many free tools are available to handle these tasks.

Here are the most common eBook formats:

- **Adobe Reader.** Readable on most computers, Web browsers, and several portable devices. PDFs are perhaps the most popular format for "free" eBooks," and other documents published online.
- **HTML.** The code used for most Web pages is also a popular eBook format, and many elements of it are used in the Kindle, Mobipocket, and EPUB formats.
- **Mobipocket.** Usable on most computers running Windows as well as several portable devices. Mobipocket, a French company, was bought by Amazon in 2005.
- **Kindle.** Amazon's proprietary format, a modified version of Mobipocket, used for the Kindle device.
- **LRF.** Sony's proprietary format used for its eReader.
- **EPUB** is an extension of the popular XML format designed to operate with different brands of software and hardware. EPUB is gaining popularity with many publishers who favor an "open," nonproprietary format. It's promoted by an industry group, the International Digital Publishing Forum. Widespread adoption of this format would enable publishers to produce and send a single file through distribution for

each book, instead of reformatting each book for different formats, advocates say.

Many publishers are concerned about Amazon's proprietary, "closed" Kindle format. If the Kindle format became as dominant in eBooks as Windows has for computers, Amazon would gain vast control over eBook pricing, these publishers fear.

Formatting your books

A variety of free software and services now exist, enabling publishers to convert their text from, for example, a Word document into the EPUB format. The Calibre software, a free product hosted at http://calibre.kovidgoyal.net, converts eBooks from 12 different formats to LRF or EPUB. Another option is BookGlutton, which hosts a free format converter at www.bookglutton.com/api.

For several years, many publishers have used Apple computers and expensive Adobe software products to edit and design books. Adobe's InDesign, a popular tool for creating pBooks and eBooks in a variety of formats, retails for $699:

www.adobe.com/products/indesign

Adobe also makes Acrobat software, which produces eBooks in the popular Portable Document Format, or PDF. It sells for about $300:

http://www.adobe.com/products/acrobat

More recently, it's become possible to publish virtually any content on an inexpensive PC using low-cost or even free software. For example, if you're already using Microsoft Word to compose your writing, you can also use it as your primary publishing tool, augmented by a few tools explored here. A good alternative to Word is OpenOffice Writer, a free software tool designed to work with PCs or Macs. The text you're reading now was composed, laid out, and edited with OpenOffice Writer. For more information, see:

http://www.openoffice.org/product/writer.html

OpenOffice Writer allows you to save your files in a wide variety of formats, including various versions of Microsoft Word, Rich Text Format, HTML, XML, and PDF. If you've used Microsoft Word, OpenOffice Writer will look familiar. A complete user's manual is available here:

http://documentation.openoffice.org/manuals/oooauthors2/0200WG-Writer-Guide.pdf

Also, Abobe offers a free online service to convert your files into PDF format:

https://createpdf.adobe.com

Go with the reflow

The PDF format was invented so that complex documents print exactly as designed, even when printed on a different brand of computer or printer. So PDF was adopted by many eBook pioneers, since it was a common, compact format. Today, however, more flexibility is needed. People are not just printing eBooks, they're reading them on a variety of devices.

One innovation, "reflowable text," enables eBook readers to adjust the size of the text, margins, and spacing. The eBook repaginates automatically, adjusting to the new display size. Plain PDFs, by contrast, contain line breaks at a certain point, so the document might be too big or too small, depending on the device where it's displayed.

So, unless you're publishing your eBook in PDF format with predefined page dimensions, your description should include a word count instead of the traditional page count. Likewise, you must remove references to certain physical page numbers you may have included in your original text.

Weave your Web

One of the best ways to ensure your intended audience discovers your book is to establish a place online, which can be a simple blog, a Web site, or an online store. There isn't a more cost-effective way to raise your profile than having your own site, which can provide a direct communications link and sales channel between you and the reader. If you sell eBooks on your site, the sales can represent nearly pure profit.

Before you begin planning your site, consider your target audience and what type of information you want to give them. Will your site be topic-driven, or personality-driven? Topic-driven sites usually work best for nonfiction, and if you continue writing related books, you'll have a built-in audience for those new books. Personality-driven sites can work well for fiction writers and those with famous names. Whatever your approach, the goal is to provide content your target audience finds worthwhile.

Some authors outsource their Web project, paying a designer thousands of dollars to build what amounts to an online brochure. That's a big mistake, because static Web sites with little content don't draw the repeat traffic that will sell your book.

Although it may seem like a daunting technical challenge, building your own site is easier than ever, thanks to improved software tools. Every major Internet hosting company now offers a variety of design templates you can use to start quickly, without having to learn computer coding. You'll gain much more from your Web site if you're the one maintaining it.

Three basic options exist for those establishing their first author site:

- **Do it yourself.** Register a domain name and build your own site. This option requires you to learn a few software tools, but provides more flexibility and control. GoDaddy.com offers fast, reliable service, and a wide variety of Web domain registration and hosting plans at competitive prices. There's no setup fee and no annual commitment is required. GoDaddy's economy plan includes 5 gigabytes of disk space, 500 e-mail accounts, forums, blogging, and photo galleries for $3.99 a month. This hosting company and most competitors such as www.Register.com offer simple tools and templates for building your own site.
- **Using a free account.** On a network such as MySpace.com, Google Pages, Blogger.com, or LiveJournal.com, a pre-packaged solution is easy to learn, but provides less flexibility. Some sites feature advertising you can't control, which can distract visitors from your message.
- **Consult a Web designer.** Find one through your local Yellow Pages, or an online firm that specializes in designing author sites. One solution is www.webforauthors.com, where new domain plans for author sites start at $168 per year.

Google Pages is an easy, free tool you can use to create Web pages quickly without having to learn HTML code. Google will host up to 100 megabytes of Web pages at no charge. To open a free account, see Pages.Google.com. Another option is FiledBy, where authors can claim a free Web page and enhance it with photos, a biography, documents, and links. See www.filedby.com

Put your site together

The great thing about a Web site is you can always add to it. Here are some basic elements you'll want to consider adding to your site:

- **Content.** Nobody will visit a site that's merely an advertisement for your book. Your content can be a series of articles, book excerpts, or even feedback from your readers.
- **Images.** Book cover artwork, description, and excerpts.
- **Your biography.**

- **Links to purchase your book.** As an affiliate, link to online retailers such as Amazon and Barnes & Noble. The more choices you offer buyers, the better.
- **Reviews of your book.**
- **Mailing list.** A form where visitors can enter their e-mail address to subscribe to a newsletter or site updates.
- **Contact information.** Your e-mail address (or a form that forwards messages) and perhaps postal address and phone number.
- **Media room.** Press releases announcing your book or any news coverage involving you or your book. Include suggested interview questions, along with your responses.

Remember that a Web site is only the start, not the end, of creating an online presence. You'll make more sales overall by offering readers a variety of ways to buy your book, from all popular content destinations. For the maximum exposure, make sure your book is available at all of the popular retailing sites, such as Amazon.

Selling content on your Web site

Selling downloadable text files or PDF documents and collecting payments with PayPal or a credit-card merchant account is one option. You can further automate the process by using one of these services:

- **ClickBank.com** collects payments, hosts your file, and enables affiliates to resell your eBook if you wish.
- **Payloadz.com** automates payments and downloads, allowing you to sell eBooks on your site or through affiliates. You can accept payment through PayPal or Google Checkout.
- **Tizra.com** is a Web-based service that lets publishers create a branded Web site from existing content. Basic accounts with up to 2,500 pages are free.
- **Payloadz.com** is a service for selling eBooks and other digital files such as music or videos. The company charges about 3 percent of the sales price plus a 30-cent fee for each transaction. Payments are handled by PayPal, which is a sub-

sidiary of the eBay online marketplace. After you upload your eBook, Payloadz stores it in a secure directory that can be accessed by special links generated when a customer pays.

- **ClickBank.com** enables publishers to sell eBooks as a one-time download or as monthly subscriptions. Customers pay using any major credit card or PayPal, and proceeds are deposited to your bank account weekly. ClickBank charges publishers a one-time activation fee of $49.95 and 7.5 percent of sales, plus a $1 fee for each transaction. The company also operates an affiliate program. Publishers determine the commission rate offered to affiliates, and ClickBank handles the accounting and payments.

- **PayPal.** Using PayPal.com, you can accept payments through your Web site, or by e-mailing buyers an invoice.

- **Google Checkout.** Although PayPal has been around longer and has more users, Checkout, launched in 2006, is backed by the search provider Google, one of the most popular Internet destinations. Checkout has the potential for revolutionizing sales of books and other items over the Internet, since purchases can be made from any participating vendor using a single Google login. Google Checkout payments are fairly easy to add to any Web site or blog, using cut-and-paste code. Google Checkout also works with Google's search advertising program, AdWords, giving advertisers an easy solution for attracting customers and processing the resulting sales.

For more information, see:

www.Checkout.Google.com

Use affiliates to drive sales

One good rule of thumb about selling things online: Give buyers as many choices as possible. If you sell eBooks directly on your Web site, it's also a good idea to mention that the same content is available on Amazon or other online retailers. If you have an affiliate account with these retailers, you can also claim a commission on your referrals.

Different readers prefer different formats and retailers. So even though you may prefer selling e-books on your Web site, some of your potential audience prefer buying paperbacks via Amazon. Your book published in an eBook format will sell more copies if it's also available in paperback. If you sell physical books through your Web site, it's also smart to include affiliate links to Amazon and Barnes & Noble on your site. Some people are just more comfortable buying from a familiar merchant. If some of your buyers are going to click over to Amazon or BN.com anyway, why not provide an affiliate link, so you can earn an extra 6 percent of the sale?

Amazon's affiliate program is called Amazon Associates. Using it, you can easily create the familiar links for your books and related products on Amazon. When your visitors click through to Amazon and make a purchase, you're paid a commission. Typically you'll receive about 6 percent, so the sale of a $20 book nets you a referral fee of $1.20.

Amazon Associates is one of the most familiar and successful programs on the Internet, with more than 1 million member sites. Under Amazon Associates' performance-based compensation plan, affiliates earn referral fees ranging from 4 percent to 8.5 percent, depending on volume. You can collect your fees in the form of a check, direct deposit, or an Amazon gift certificate.

Besides providing Amazon Associates links to specific books, you can display Amazon banner ads or search boxes on your site, and you'll earn referral fees on sales resulting from those clicks.

After your visitors click on your Associates link, you'll receive commissions not only on book purchases, but most other purchases those customers make during the following 24 hours. For example, if your visitor also buys a big-screen TV, you'll get a commission for that big-ticket item.

Besides the plain Amazon Associates product links, Amazon offers a contextual program called Omakase, which displays different products based on the content on your site and your visitor's browsing history at Amazon. The advantage for affiliates is that Omakase is dynamic, exposing your audience to different books each time they visit a different page on your site, increasing the odds of a purchase.

The name Omakase is Japanese for "Leave it up to us," a custom in Japanese restaurants in which the chef improvises a meal based on his knowledge of the diner's preferences.

For more information, visit:

www.amazon.com/associates

Multimedia tools

As wireless and home high-speed Internet service becomes more common, audio and video content are becoming valuable tools for online book promotion. Multimedia is particularly effective for niche authors and newcomers who haven't attracted mainstream media coverage.

Multimedia grabs the attention of younger people who spend more leisure time online, while consuming less traditional media like newspapers and television. Meanwhile, production and distribution of trailers is getting easier and cheaper by the day, thanks to inexpensive video cameras and free hosting sites like www.YouTube.com.

Book trailers, an increasingly popular tool for book publicity, often resemble movie previews, music videos, or talk shows. Even though trailers are promotional materials, the people who choose to watch often perceive them as interesting, valuable content.

For an author or publisher, trailers can serve as an infomercial, a message that appears on a cable network of 5 million channels—except you have global reach and minimal expense. The videos contain a "buy this book" link to Amazon or the publisher's site, prompting impulse purchases from viewers, which can make an effective trailer instantly profitable.

VidLit.com produces slick trailers using animation, narration, and background music. The clips can be hosted on the author's blog or Web site, or e-mailed to newsletter subscribers. As part of its service, VidLit.com can forward trailers to literary bloggers who often post the videos.

Successful trailers are an example of viral marketing because of the huge exposure gained through Web links and e-mails. Thanks largely to e-mail forwarding, a trailer for the humor book *Yiddish with Dick and Jane* was seen by 1 million people during its first week, helping to sell 150,000 copies of the book. You can view the video at:

www.VidLit.com/yidlit

Do-it-yourself videos are another option, thanks to falling prices of digital camcorders. Video clips are an effective tool for authors unable to finance a bookstore tour, or whose disparate audience makes touring impractical. If you have a PC with Windows XP, you can edit digital video yourself using a free program in your Accessories folder called "Movie Maker." If you're a Mac user, there's iMovie.

Author Chris Epting scored big using YouTube to promote his 2007 book *Led Zeppelin Crashed Here*, a guide to "rock and roll landmarks." Six months before publication, Epting began posting a series of trailers, featuring photos he shot for the book backed with classic-rock soundtracks. The videos prompted thousands of rock fans to write to Epting with suggestions for the book, as well as requests to buy it. Closer to his publication date, Epting posted interactive videos and a trivia contest. You can view the videos here:

www.youtube.com/view_play_list?p=FA5F436AF546723F

Fish for readers with podcasts

Sales of digital audio are expanding rapidly, fueled by the increased popularity of portable music players such as the iPod, and eBook readers such as Amazon's Kindle, which can also play audio files. A good way to get started with audio content is by podcasting.

The best way to get a feel for podcasting is to sample some of the content available:

- **Podiobooks:** Podiobooks.com. Serialized audiobooks. Authors can sign up to distribute the books (or books in progress) here. The site asks listeners to donate $9.99 per title. Podiobooks keeps 25 percent to cover its expenses and passes the remaining revenue to authors.
- **iTunes:** www.Apple.com/itunes/podcasts. Here you can sample or subscribe to podcasts.
- **Yahoo Podcasts:** Podcasts.yahoo.com. Listen to podcasts using your Web browser, or download files.
- **LibriVox:** Librivox.org. Free audiobooks from the public domain.

Audio recordings you may already have—such as interviews or book-readings—can be repurposed as a podcast, providing Internet users with yet another way to discover you and your book.

Some podcasts are a recurring feature, sometimes called a podioBook. Perhaps you'll decide to provide your audio content for free to help generate word of mouth for your book. Some authors create value-added podcasts and charge subscription fees.

To record material for your podcasts, all that's required is a micro-phone and PC. Free software for recording and editing podcasts is offered at www.Audacity.Sourceforge.net. Another option is www.HipCast.com, which lets you create podcasts through your Web browser or telephone, then post it to your blog or Web site. For Mac users, GarageBand is a good podcast tool.

One easy way to get started quickly with podcasting is to set up a free account at Podbean.com. Another option for free podcasting hosting is Mypodcast.com.

Here's a more complete guide for making your own podcasts:

www.How-To-Podcast-Tutorial.com

Learn how to create podcasts and upload them to iTunes at this address:

www.apple.com/itunes/whatson/podcasts/creatorfaq.html

Traditionally, audiobooks were an afterthought, with lackluster marketing and meager sales. But that is changing as gadgets like the iPod and iPhone make buying and listening to audio content easy. Providing a free bonus of digital content is another option for publishers. For example, Chris Anderson, author of *Free: The Past and Future of a Radical Price*, has suggested that in the future, audiobooks might be given away free with the pBook edition.

Using the iTunes Affiliate Program, you can place links on your Web site to the iTunes Store. You can link to your audiobooks, podcasts, and iPhone and iPod touch applications. In addition to your regular revenue, you earn a 5 percent affiliate commission on revenue generated by the links posted on your site.

Apply for the iTunes Affiliate Program here:

www.apple.com/storeaffiliates

All links to iTunes launch the iTunes software and open to the iTunes Store. If visitors to your site don't have iTunes installed, the link forwards the browser to a site where they can download iTunes.

Thanks to the ease of digital recording and distribution, audio content is becoming an additional revenue generator for authors. Audio can be sold through Amazon's CreateSpace as downloadable files or compact discs. Another distribution option is Audible.com, which sells digital audiobooks on Amazon, iTunes, and other sites. In some cases Audible will buy the audio rights to your book and perform the recording. In other cases, Audible.com buys prerecorded programs. Contact the company via e-mail at content@audible.com, providing a description of your existing content and content you plan to produce over the next six months.

Get more feedback

Another way to improve your writing while generating a fan base is to use "beta readers," an increasingly popular technique for fiction writers. For example, at FanFiction.net, writers upload hundreds of stories and novels daily, in various stages of completion. A great way to hone your writing chops is by recruiting beta readers, and getting their reactions to your work.

Often, authors don't know their beta readers personally, but still acknowledge their contributions in the finished book. Some beta readers specialize in critiquing grammar and other mechanical aspects of writing, while other readers advise on story structure, logic or character development. For more information:

www.fanfiction.net/betareaders

www.absolutewrite.com/forums

Wag the Long Tail

One of the beautiful things about digital content is you can make your work available instantly to virtually anyone in the world. But that doesn't necessarily mean people will find it.

Amazon, with its 90 million registered buyers, provides free worldwide exposure for your book. And just as importantly, thanks to its book-recommendation feature, Amazon shows your book to those readers most likely to buy it. Also, Amazon's book reviews, written by customers, can provide important exposure for your eBook. Put simply, you can use Amazon to level the field between you and publishers with the deepest pockets.

Amazon helps create demand for niche eBooks that have a widely dispersed audience that can't be targeted effectively through traditional marketing. Twenty-five percent of Amazon's sales come from obscure books that aren't even carried in a Barnes & Noble superstore stocking 100,000 titles. And the percentage of these "long tail" sales grows every year. The attraction for book buyers is being able to find exactly what they want, says Chris Anderson, author of the business bestseller *The Long Tail: Why the Future of Business is Selling Less of More*. For 50 years, publishers have been chasing blockbusters—the bestseller hits. They had to, because with limited shelf space, bookstores had to focus on the stuff that moved fastest. Today, chasing blockbusters is obsolete. Authors and publishers have a wide-open opportunity in serving niches.

These niche books are the ones people care about most, and the ones Amazon is most effective in recommending. And eBooks offer the best opportunity because costs can be cut to the bone.

Unlike a traditional paper-bound book, eBooks don't necessarily require outside editors, copy editors, cover designers, proofreaders, or typesetters.

Each of Amazon's 90 million customers sees a unique store. The layout is personalized, based on which books the customer previously viewed or purchased. Each customer has a recommendations list, based on which books are bought most frequently by other customers with similar buying histories.

If you have an Amazon account, view your recommendations here:

www.Amazon.com/yourstore

As more people buy your eBook on Amazon, it becomes easier for future customers to discover it. When Amazon notices your book is selling, it's automatically displayed higher in search results and category lists. And most importantly, Amazon begins inserting your title into book recommendations on its Web site and in e-mails to customers.

Book recommendations are Amazon's second-biggest sales engine, after keyword searches. Sixty-six percent of sales are to returning customers, many of them acting on automated recommendations for books popular with customers with similar buying histories.

Because they are personalized, Amazon's recommendations are network-powered word of mouth—more effective than a highway billboard seen by everyone in town. And as long as your book keeps selling, Amazon continues recommending it month after month, year after year, to its likely audience.

Amazon displays book recommendations in several places:

- On Amazon's home page, where it says, "Hello, [NAME], we have recommendations for you. Click here to view all your book recommendations."
- In e-mails titled Amazon.com Recommends ... and New for You, periodically sent to Amazon customers.
- In a book's Frequently Bought Together list. Every book's detail page on Amazon includes this list, which shows several other books bought most frequently by customers who also purchased the displayed book.

- An extended Also-Bought list that includes many more titles is accessible from each book's detail page at the link "Explore similar items." Buyers can view the same list during the checkout process by viewing "Customers who bought [Title] also bought..."

Amazon Sales Rank

An important barometer of your success on Amazon—and a great source of competitive intelligence—is the Amazon Sales Rank, which is found in the "Product Details" section of each item for sale. Amazon Sales Rank shows the relative sales volume of each book compared with every other title. Updated hourly, the system assigns a unique rank to each eBook relative to other titles' sales, with the top-selling book ranked 1.

The closer your rank gets to 1, the more often your book appears in Amazon recommendations. Your book's Amazon Sales Rank is public evidence of the success of your book. Many booksellers, publishers, and agents pay close attention to Amazon ranks. So if you manage to pump up the sales rank of your book, it can prompt brick-and-mortar stores to order more copies. Publishers looking for a complementary title might ask you to write the book for them.

One independent Web site, Titlez.com, allows users to instantly retrieve historic and current Amazon rankings and create printable reports with 7-day, 30-day, 90-day, and lifetime averages. This allows you to see how book topic areas or individual titles perform over time relative to others.

Titlez is a handy tool for evaluating topic ideas because you can gauge the potential audience for a given topic or title. Using Titlez you can easily assemble a list of related books with their historical sales rankings and descriptions. This indicates whether other books on the topic have succeeded or failed, and may show where opportunities exist or where markets are saturated.

Titlez also provides pricing information on competitive titles, helping you determine the right price for your book. You can also track your book's performance over time to assess the effect of promotional efforts and marketing programs.

Online book reviews

Positive reviews on Amazon boost your sales not only on Amazon, but everywhere people buy books. A great way to get more reviews for your eBook on Amazon is to find several dozen readers in your target audience and give each of them a copy of your eBook.

Remember that many readers aren't yet accustomed to eBooks, so you should always offer a printed version to potential reviewers as well.

Will giving away several dozen copies of your book detract from sales? Perhaps you'll lose a sale or two, but you'll gain much more from word of mouth. The initial readers who enjoy your book will recommend it to friends, and those new readers will recommend it to more.

Once your book is selling, you'll have a steady stream of potential reviewers. Whenever you receive e-mails from readers with praise for your book or requests for further information, you might conclude your response this way:

> *Thank you for the kind words about my book. If you ever have a spare moment, it would be a great help if you could post a review of it on Amazon and let other potential readers know why you liked it. It's not necessary to write a lengthy, formal review—a summary of the comments you sent me would be fine. Here's a link to the review form for my book:*
>
> *http://www.Amazon.com/gp/customer-reviews/write-a-review.html?asin=ASIN*

The link at the end of the message takes the reader to Amazon's Web form for book reviews. To customize the link for your book, replace the last four characters, ASIN, with your book's Amazon identification number, which is specified in the "Product Details" section of your book's page on Amazon.

Negative reviews are part of the territory. You can't please everyone. Unduly harsh or insulting reviews are often deleted by Amazon when the offensive review is brought to the attention of its Community Help department, community-help@amazon.com. So it pays to familiarize yourself with Amazon's review guidelines:

http://www.amazon.com/review/guidelines/review-guidelines.html

Amapedia

Amazon's Amapedia feature enables customers to write their own articles, or "wikis," on any product page. This collection of Amazon customer-written content, based at Amapedia.com, resembles Wikipedia.org, a popular online encyclopedia.

The concept behind wikis is that anyone can write one and publish it quickly, then anyone else can come along later and correct mistakes. Wikis are supposed to differ from customer reviews and other types of user-generated content in one important way: Writers are supposed to stick to facts, and avoid injecting their opinions.

What could undermine the utility of wikis is their misuse by spammers. And there's nothing to prevent competing authors or publishers from adding false information. Wikis are supposed to be self-correcting, but experience shows this doesn't always happen.

For more information, see:

http://amapedia.amazon.com

Expose yourself on social networks

The "Customer Discussions" feature enables Amazon users to ask questions, share insights, and give opinions about products. One of the many possible uses of this feature might be to provide a forum for a manufacturer or seller to notify shoppers of a new product feature or other current information. You can subscribe to receive notifications from Amazon whenever new questions or responses are posted to a particular discussion.

To see the Customer Discussions for a particular item, scroll down the item detail page to the section "Customer Discussions."

Another valuable source of free publicity is Internet social networks such as MySpace and Facebook. Although many of the so-called "friends" on these popular sites have never met in person, the resulting social networks have some of the same network characteristics as real flesh-and-blood "social networks." The attractive thing for authors is that MySpace and the other sites can generate real word of mouth for your books.

Musical artists were among the first content creators to discover how to attract a larger audience by setting up a free account at MySpace.com. The bands put samples of their music on their MySpace "profile," and asked friends to forward invitations to an ever-bigger circle of like-minded friends. Likewise, thousands of authors have used MySpace to attract more readers. Horror novelist Michael Laimo was interviewed in several print publications after reporters noticed his MySpace page. He got his first movie deal through MySpace after an independent director sent him a message asking about film rights. And hundreds of fans have told him they bought his books after seeing his MySpace profile:

www.MySpace.com/MichaelLaimo

There are several ways to find people on MySpace who might be in your target audience—by searching for murder mysteries, historical romance, self-improvement, organic food, or whatever topics your eBook touches on. Perhaps there's a famous writer whose style you emulate, and you'd like to find other admirers. Once you've found potential friends, you can send a request for them to "add" you as a friend. The invitee can accept, decline, or ignore your request, although most people accept.

Once you're friends with someone on MySpace, you can post comments on each other's profile pages and see each other's full circle of friends.

Some authors create a separate MySpace profile dedicated to each new eBook they write, using the book title as the profile name. After creating the profile, these authors often send bulletins to all their friends, requesting that they add their new book's profile to their friends list, getting more exposure. For fiction authors, creating a MySpace profile for a fictional character can be an attention grabber.

MySpace is just one of a growing number of social-networking sites. Google owns another of these sites, Orkut.com. Facebook.com is more popular than ever. Another networking hub is Ning.com, where you can devise and host your own social network.

Twitter.com is a micro-blogging service enabling users to send and read other members' updates, or "tweets," which are text messages up to 140 characters long. Senders can restrict delivery to their friends, or send tweets to everyone. The service has been wildly popular with tech-savvy users.

Social networks for book readers

LibraryThing.com was launched in 2005 and instantly became the No. 1 social-networking site devoted to bibliophiles. Like other popular social networks, LibraryThing has grown purely on word of mouth, not advertising.

Like other social book-cataloging sites, part of the fun at LibraryThing is belonging to a big club that lets you display how eclectic and singular your taste is. Meanwhile there's the chance you'll meet a few one-in-a-million literary soul mates who are passionate about the same books as you.

Spending time on LibraryThing is addictive because of all the interesting connections that surface, especially with obscure books. Entering your copy of Harry Potter won't move the needle. But when you enter your copy of *Environmental Kuznet Curves*, things get interesting.

Members enter their book collection simply by punching in the ISBNs. Then members can compare their whole collection—or individual rarities—against the collections of others. Ever wonder who else in the world has read that oddball book you love? On LibraryThing you'll know.

LibraryThing also has a book recommendation system that founder Tim Spalding claims is more accurate than Amazon's, simply because its users pay more attention. On LibraryThing, members input the books they want to drive their recommendations, no matter when or where they acquired them. Books you've purchased as gifts easily corrupt Amazon recommendations, and most users don't input the books they've purchased elsewhere.

LibraryThing also has a user-driven tagging system, which public libraries can incorporate with their online catalogs. Unfortunately, LibraryThing has been slow to adapt to eBooks.

Shelfari.com is somewhat similar to LibraryThing, where users build virtual bookshelves of the volumes they've read, and can review, rate, tag, and discuss those books. Amazon bought Shelfari in 2008, and pipes in customer reviews and book-buying links.

Check out the digital library

The exciting thing about eBooks is the potential for interconnectedness using Internet tools sometimes known as "Web 2.0." This participatory environment allows readers to comment on, and even collaborate on, writing projects.

One of the simplest of these collaborative tools is tagging. It's an increasingly common way for Internet users to organize things by using personal keywords. Tags can be used to label all kinds of items, including eBooks, Web pages, and pictures. Already, some are calling tags "the Internet's Dewey Decimal System." Tags are public annotations, a user-defined category name or keyword.

For example, with a book like *Gone With the Wind*, you might assign tags like "Civil War," "fiction," "epic," and "romance." It all depends on what the book means to you.

You can view all your tags on Amazon here:

www.Amazon.com/gp/tagging/manage-tags

Users create tags for their own purposes, but they can be used by anyone. With enough people participating, tags can become an effortless, super-accurate recommendations system among like-minded people. Amazon and some library catalogs have introduced user-generated tags to supplement hierarchical systems, like Library of Congress subject headings.

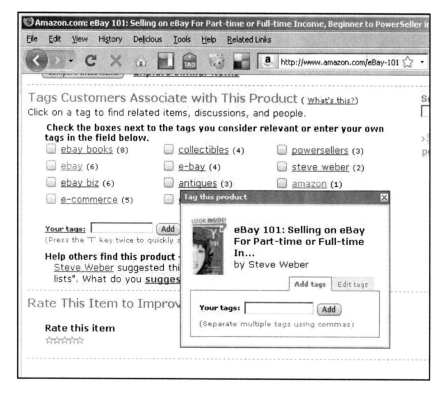

Amazon's "tag this product" window allows users to assign their own descriptive words or phrases to books and other products.

Here you can add or delete tags, and designate them public or private. You can view the tags for any Amazon customer who's made at least one purchase, unless they've chosen to keep their tags private.

An easy way to monitor the Amazon tags that interest you is to subscribe to a "feed" of the tags using a reader such as Bloglines.com or Google Reader.

For example, let's imagine you want to be notified each time an Amazon user tags a book (or other product) using the tag "historical fiction." Go to the page for the tag:

www.amazon.com/tag/historical fiction

A "tag cloud" displaying the most commonly used tags by customers at Amazon.com. At a glance, you can see which are most popular, and click on the tag to navigate Amazon products. Tags are an alternate, more "democratic" navigation tool than hierarchical systems, such as company-defined categories.

You'll see a display of the items most often tagged "historical fiction" by Amazon customers. Scroll down to the bottom right corner of the page and click the link for "Subscribe – RSS Feed."

Another way you can use the RSS feed: Embed a widget on your own Web site to display the most popular Amazon products for a tag, and earn affiliate commissions for clicks resulting in purchases through the Amazon Associates program.

The feed will also inform you of new "community discussions" or Amazon guides or Listmanias about historical romance. You'll want to monitor these so you can immediately discover when someone mentions your book or topic area on Amazon.

Another tagging method feature on Amazon is tied directly to its keyword search feature (the small window where shoppers can search by title, author name, or other words). "Tags for Search" enables anyone with an Amazon account—seller or buyer—to add a bit of human intelligence to the site's search engine. On each product detail page, the link "Help others find this product—tag it for Amazon search" allows users to recommend tying a product to specific keywords. Users also explain why the keywords are relevant and will help people find the item. Then Amazon customers searching for those keywords will see your book in search results.

One way you can take advantage of Tags for Search is to link your book with relevant words and expressions that don't appear in the title. For example, let's imagine you sell a book about predicting hurricanes. A year after your book goes on the market, the most damaging hurricane in history, a storm named Zelda, devastates the Florida coast. By entering the Search Suggestion "Hurricane Zelda," more buyers would find your book, even though it didn't contain the word "Zelda."

Once your Search Suggestion is approved, when customers search using your keywords, the product appears in search results along with your relevancy explanation.

You can also tag books within a personalized section of Amazon called Your Media Library:

www.Amazon.com/gp/library

Amazon's Web page for the tag "historical fiction," which is located at www.amazon.com/tags/historical fiction, enables you to monitor related books, lists, guides, and discussions.

Here you can view all your previous purchases, access Kindle books you've purchased, and buy online access to eligible physical books you've purchased from Amazon, using the "Amazon Upgrade" feature. You can organize your Media Library by tagging individual books:

- Click on the book to select it. Bibliographic information will be displayed at the top of the screen.
- Any currently used tags for the book will be displayed just below.
- Click the Add button to enter tags. If you've created other tags previously, a list of similar tags is shown below the edit box.

- Type in a new tag or click a suggested tag and click OK to save.

Although it's relatively new, Media Library could become the hub of Amazon's social-networking strategy, an avenue for readers to connect with others who have common interests.

> *When books are deeply linked, you'll be able to click on the title in any bibliography or any footnote and find the actual book referred to in the footnote. The books referenced in that book's bibliography will themselves be available, and so you can hop through the library in the same way we hop through Web links, traveling from footnote to footnote to footnote until you reach the bottom of things.*
>
> —Kevin Kelly, *Scan This Book!*
> http://www.kk.org/writings/scan_this_book.php

Amazon's Listmanias lists allow any Amazon user—customers, authors, sellers, music lovers, movie buffs—to create lists of their favorite items organized by theme. Listmanias appear in various places on Amazon, like product detail pages and alongside search results. Listmanias that mention your product can expose it to thousands of potential customers on Amazon, and the list can even appear in Google search results for associated keywords.

Listmanias are ranked by popularity among shoppers, based on viewership and the number of votes calling it "helpful." See the 100 most popular Listmanias here:

http://www.Amazon.com/gp/richpub/listmania/toplists

Niche products stand to gain the most from Listmanias. The more focused a Listmania is, the more helpful it is to buyers hungry for specific information—so the more likely it is to be noticed, read carefully, and acted on. To write a Listmania, click on the link at the bottom of your Amazon profile page, "More to Explore." Or start your list by clicking on the link "Create Your Own List" on an existing Listmania.

Raise your profile

By default, each Amazon account holder has a "profile" page. If you have an Amazon account, you can see your profile at:

www.Amazon.com/gp/pdp

If you've never used any of Amazon's community features, your profile will be mostly blank. After you become more active, your Amazon profile is a convenient place to access and manage content you've posted to Amazon, like book reviews, Listmanias, blog posts, and So You'd Like to ... guides.

For book authors, an Amazon profile provides a great opportunity to educate shoppers about your titles, and to refer them to your own Web site if you wish. You can upload your photograph, post a short biography, and add several personal details.

If you have an Amazon Connect blog, your posts are displayed on your Amazon profile, along with some anonymous feedback from readers, such as "5 of 6 readers who voted liked this post."

On the right column of your profile, you can set preferences for display of your Amazon wish lists and previous purchases. By default, your previous Amazon purchases are publicly viewable, but you can make them private.

Rise above the noise

In this age of information overload, the best way to sell your writing is to give some of it away. As an author, you're competing for attention with millions of other new books, video games, sports, music, and endless other distractions. Publishing free chapters and sample content sparks your creative juices, draws more readers, and burnishes your reputation. Here's how to get it done:

- **Post question-and-answer content.** On your blog or Web site, summarize the best questions you receive from readers via e-mail, phone calls, letters, or personal conversations. Publish them in a question-and-answer format. This provides interesting, valuable and easy-to-read content. Q&A content is simple to produce, especially after you've generated raw material by answering e-mails. When you post this content publicly, all your readers benefit, not just one. Q&As expand your audience because the format boosts your visibility with search engines. Many people searching the Web actually type questions into Google, such as "How to make orchids bloom." You can rewrite the questions for clarity, or even generate the question yourself to help illustrate a point.
- **Offer book excerpts or sample chapters.** Make this available as a PDF document on your Web site or blog. At a minimum, you should offer your book's table of contents, index and a short excerpt.

One popular science-fiction author, Cory Doctorow, provides free downloads of the entire text of all his novels at his Web site, CrapHound.com. The resulting publicity far outweighs the cost of any lost book sales, and, he adds: "The biggest threat to new authors isn't piracy, it's obscurity." For more details on Doctorow's experiences in providing free eBooks, read his essay titled "Giving it Away" here:

http://www.forbes.com/2006/11/30/cory-doctorow-copyright-tech-media_cz_cd_books06_1201doctorow.html

- **Participate in online discussions.** Answering queries about your area of expertise on message boards and e-mail lists can can lure more readers. At the bottom of all your messages and e-mails, add a signature with your Web address and current book title.
- **Post comments on blogs related to your topic.** Most blogs allow you to include a link back to your site in your comment. Invest the time in providing useful, thoughtful commentary, and you'll gain new readers.

Blog for attention

Blogging is a relatively easy way for you to publicize your book and improve your writing. If you can write an e-mail, you can write a blog—it's the easiest, cheapest, and perhaps best way for authors to find an audience and connect with readers.

The main thing that distinguishes a blog from a plain old Web site is that a blog is frequently updated with short messages, or posts. Readers often chime in with their own comments at the bottom of each post. This free exchange of ideas is what makes blogs a revolutionary tool for authors: A successful blog is a constant stream of ideas, inspiration, perspective, and advice—it's a real-time, global focus group.

Compared with other types of Internet publicity content such as static Web sites or e-mail newsletters, blogs provide three big advantages:

- Blogs are easy to start and maintain.
- The short, serialized content of blogs encourages regular readership, repeated exposure to your books, and more sales.
- Blogs rank high in search-engine results from Google and other providers, making them easy to find.

You can find a list of the most popular blogs here:

www.Technorati.com/pop/blogs

Another good place to browse and search blogs is:

www.blogsearch.google.com

Once you've found a few blogs of interest, it's easy to find more. Bloggers tend to link to one another, both within their blog posts, and often within a side menu of links known as a blogroll.

A handy tool for keeping track of all your blogs is a news-reader or aggregator, which saves you the trouble of poking around the Web, looking for new blog posts. Instead, your news-reader gathers and displays updates for you. One free, easy-to-use reader is:

www.bloglines.com

Good blogs are addictive, which is one reason they're so effective for authors. Many book buyers must be exposed to a title six or seven times before deciding to buy. With a good blog, getting repeated exposure won't be a problem.

A lively blog is like a focus group and writing laboratory rolled into one: It provides you with constant feedback, criticism, and new ideas. Indeed, the true power of blogging is the momentum created by your audience. Once your blog has 100 frequent readers, it has critical mass.

Amazon's "Connect" feature enables you to blog on Amazon's site, with snippets from your blog appearing on your book product pages. It's a unique opportunity to communicate with new readers.

You can also use your Amazon blog to refer visitors to your own Web site. Some authors do this by posting only the first paragraph of their post at Amazon, and asking readers to click through to their own site to continue reading.

You can get more information and apply for an Amazon blog here:

www.amazon.com/connect

One fast way to add content to your Amazon Connect blog is by re-purposing material you've already generated elsewhere, through e-mails or other writing.

Creating blog posts

A free, easy way to find new raw material for your blog is to create a Google Alert, which will automatically scour thousands of media sources for any keywords you specify. You'll be alerted via e-mail when something containing your keywords appears in newspapers, magazines, Web sites, or other sources. Sign up at:

www.Google.com/alerts

Google Alerts are also a handy way to monitor mentions of your blog title, book titles, and even your name or the names of other authors. To search for words that appear in an exact order, such as your book title, enclose the words in quotation marks.

The essential ingredient of a blog is its short entries, or posts. They're arranged in reverse chronological order, with the newest at top. Posts can be a few sentences long, or many paragraphs long, and often link to outside information like blogs, newspaper stories, or multimedia clips hosted elsewhere on the Web.

Nearly any tidbit of information relevant to your audience can be spun into a blog post of some type:

- **Informational.** A news-oriented blurb. A new development.
- **Question/Answer.** Easy to write, and fun to read. Reliable material, even if you have to make up the question.
- **Instructional.** Can be a longer post, a tutorial that explains how to do something related to your niche.
- **Link posts.** Find an interesting blog post elsewhere. Link to it and add your own spin.
- **Rant.** Let off some steam, and let it rip. Interesting blogs don't play it safe, they take sides.
- **Book review.** Review a book related to your field. It can be a new book or a classic unfamiliar to newcomers.

- **Product reviews.** The word "review" is a popular search term. Give your frank opinion, and encourage your readers to chime in with their own views.
- **Lists.** Write about the "Top 5 Ways" to do a task, or the "Top 10 Reasons" for such-and-such. Readers love lists. If someone else publishes a list, you can summarize it or critique it on your own blog.
- **Interviews.** Chat with someone in your field. Provide a text summary on your blog. You can also add a transcript or even an audio file.
- **Case studies.** Report on how so-and-so does such-and-such. You don't have to call it a "case study," just tell the story.
- **Profiles.** Profiles focus on a particular person, a personality. The person profiled can be someone well known in your field, or perhaps a newcomer nobody knows.

Blow your horn

Landing national media exposure can greatly enhance your book sales, but many new authors don't have the resources to hire a publicist. One way to get exposure in newspapers, radio, and television without hiring a publicist is PRLeads.com. Several times a day, users receive a list of queries from journalists looking for expert sources for the stories they're writing.

On a typical day, a PRLeads subscriber might see a query like this:

SUBJECT:

BUSINESS : Small Companies Going into International Markets – Boston Daily News

For a national newspaper, I'm writing a story on how small-business owners should make the decision to go into international markets. What factors should they consider? How can they evaluate the opportunity? How soon after establishing yourself domestically should you consider this? I'm looking for comments from experts, and examples of entrepreneurs who have been dealing with this issue.

Authors and other experts with relevant expertise could send this reporter a brief e-mail, describing their credentials and how they can address the topic. Later the reporter might follow up via phone or e-mail for an interview. Subscriptions to PRLeads cost $99 a month. For more information, see:

www.PRLeads.com/pr-leads-faq.htm

An increasingly popular free alternative to PRLeads is Help-A-Reporter-Online, or HARO. The service e-mails you tips about stories being written by reporters at newspapers, magazines, blogs, and TV, and what experts they want to interview. See:

http://helpareporter.com

Here's a typical lead from HARO:

> *Summary: Need water conservation expert*
> *Category: General*
> *Name: Jane Doe*
> *Email: jane_doe@e-mail.net*
> *Title: Writer*
> *Media Outlet/Publication: Trade Publication*
> *Anonymous? No*
> *Specific Geographic Region? No*
> *Deadline: 12:00 PM PACIFIC - February 19*
>
> *Query:*
> *"I'm looking for an expert to provide tips for water con-servation for amusement parks/resorts."*

Pay cash for new eyeballs

Pay-per-click advertising, or PPC, has revolutionized online promotion, and has been wonderfully effective for many Internet businesses. The prime advantage of PPC is its ability to deliver your ad to targeted audiences.

Unlike with most advertising, with pay-per-click you don't pay fees each time your ad is displayed, but only when someone clicks on your ad and is taken to your Web site. Although PPC can bring targeted traffic to your site, it's seldom cost-effective unless you are selling a high-priced book. Google, for example, might charge you from 75 cents to $20 or more for competitive keywords, and only a tiny fraction of those clicks will result in sales.

In the early days of PPC advertising, Google AdWords and Yahoo Search Marketing were about the only vehicles. Back then PPC was often called "search engine advertising" because ads were always displayed alongside search results at Google, Yahoo, or another search engine. Sometimes the only thing differentiating your ad from an unpaid search result was the small label "Sponsored Link."

PPC is considered a revolutionary way of advertising because you spend money to attract people who have already expressed an interest in what you are selling. In the past several years, Google seems to have perfected PPC with its AdWords program. Not only are ads shown alongside search results, but they also pop up on millions of Web sites—relevant blogs, commerce sites, forums, etc.

Google AdWords

With Google AdWords, advertisers write short three-line text ads, then bid on keywords relevant to their ad. The ads appear alongside relevant search results or on content pages. For example, to advertise a tropical fish store, you might bid on several different keywords and phrases—aquarium, exotic fish, fishkeeping, and pet fish.

A Google search for "self publish iphone" returns an Adwords advertisement in the shaded area under the search box. Below are Web sites containing those words, in the order judged most relevant by Google.

Depending on how popular those words and phrases are with other advertisers, the more you'll pay for each click. The higher your bid, the higher your ad appears on the relevant page.

The most familiar PPC ads are the ubiquitous Google "Sponsored Links" that appear alongside search results or on content-related Web sites.

Learn more about Google's AdWords program at:

http://adwords.google.com

Pay to play on Amazon

Because advertisers have driven up the bidding on many popular pay-per-click keywords, PPC isn't a particularly effective way to sell individual low-priced items on popular networks like Google. More recently, Amazon has introduced its own PPC network called Product Ads. Advertisers bid against one another for space in the Amazon category where they want their ads to appear. The higher the bid, the more exposure an ad receives.

Product Ad links may appear in Amazon detail pages or search results. Customers who click on the links are forwarded to the advertiser's Web address. One convenient feature with Product Ads is that you can upload a list of items you want to promote, instead of manually creating an ad for each one. Product Ads may be displayed in these categories: Electronics & Computers, Home & Garden, Tools, and Toys, Kids & Baby. For more information, see:

http://www.amazonservices.com/productAds/

Buy X, Get Y

You can increase the odds of buyers finding your eBook at Amazon by paying $750 a month to display it with a complementary item in a program called Buy X, Get Y, known as BXGY. The primary benefit is that your product's name and a thumbnail image of it are prominently displayed on the detail page of a related item under the heading Best Value. Customers who buy both items get an additional 5 percent discount.

You'll pay more for a pairing with popular items. For example, Amazon charges $1,000 a month for pairing with a book with a sales rank of 1 to 250, and $750 a month for pairing with slower-selling books with ranks exceeding 250.

An ideal BXGY campaign would pair your item with Amazon's No. 1 bestseller in the same category, if that bestseller appealed precisely to your target market. The stronger the Amazon Sales Rank of the paired title, the more people will see your promotion, and the more traffic will be redirected to your book's detail page. But if the paired item isn't relevant to yours, it won't work. For example, pairing your book with an installment of Harry Potter might bring a ton of exposure, but it wouldn't produce many sales, unless your book appealed to precisely the same audience.

You can find BXGY candidates by browsing Amazon's category best-seller lists and searching Amazon for related keywords. Use the "Sort by" drop-down menu on the right to sift products according to sales rank, publication date, and price. You can also browse for potential pairings by visiting this link and clicking on the appropriate category:

http://www.amazon.com/gp/bestsellers

The main value of BXGY is sending readers to your item's detail page who might not find it otherwise. You can pair your item with only one other title at a time. Publishers can participate in BXGY under Amazon's "small vendor" program if they have less than $1 million in annual sales on Amazon by applying at:

http://www.Amazon.com/exec/obidos/subst/misc/co-op/small-vendor-faq.html

Graduate to print

After you've established a successful formula with eBooks, you can use digital printing to add readers and revenue. Ultimately many more people will read and buy your pBook because paper is still the most popular format among readers. Just as eBooks provide a gateway to publishing, digital printing is the smartest, lowest-risk way to expand into physical books.

Not long ago, conventional print publishing required a big cash outlay, but digital technology enables small print jobs. With digital Print on Demand, or POD, books are printed after customers pay, so you incur no upfront inventory or storage costs.

Two main ways to proceed into POD are:

- **Author service.** Using an author service, you'll pay a premium for convenience. The disadvantage is you'll probably pay inflated printing costs, which are often obscured. Depending on which company you choose, you'll pay from $200 to several thousand dollars for a bundle of services including typesetting, cover design, editing, and perhaps more. The editing, proofreading, and design services are likely to be mediocre or worse. The most popular providers are Amazon's CreateSpace, Lulu.com, BookLocker, and iUniverse. No matter which company is used, authors are frequently disappointed because they expect more sales than they actually get.

- **Publisher service.** Using a publisher service is less expensive in the long run, but is more difficult, especially for first-time publishers. You'll probably have to learn how to format and upload your own files or arrange for a freelancer to do it. The advantage with this route is you'll usually pay less for printing, and you'll have more control over pricing. So if your book is a good seller, you'll earn more money this way, perhaps much more. With POD, or Print on Demand, the major players are Lightning Source, Replica, and Book-Surge, an Amazon subsidiary

Be skeptical of companies that offer "bargain" pricing, like packages including cover design, typesetting, and editing for just a few hundred dollars. The quality of the job will likely be poor, with a cookie-cutter cover design, and "editing" outsourced to someone without superior English skills. Likewise, avoid companies offering a deal "this week only," which is usually a sign of pressure sales techniques, not a good deal.

First-time publishers usually aren't aware of three key disadvantages of author-service firms:

- **Lack of control over pricing and discounts.** The author-service company, not you, usually decides the retail price of the book, generally depending on the size of your book and which package of services you bought.
- **No branding control.** Depending on which services you buy, the company's name, such as CreateSpace or Lulu, might appear as the publisher of record. This might detract from your book's credibility if shoppers conclude this represents "amateur" authors, not professionals.
- **No competition to sell your book.** If your book is available through a wholesaler, booksellers will compete to sell it at close to the wholesale price. By contrast, if your book is available through an author-service firm, it's usually sold at full list price, with no competition. This is a turnoff for most buyers, who expect a discount from the list price, especially on Amazon.

It pays to shop around. Some of the author-services companies have terrible reputations, like the "author mills" of the 20th century that lured first-time writers with advertisements in the back of magazines. Just like traditional publishers, these service companies can take an excruciatingly long time to get your book on the market.

If you sign with any author-services company, read the contract carefully. Ensure that you will retain all rights to your work, so you can switch to a different printer if you want. At a minimum, make sure the deal includes distribution—you want your book made available through Amazon and a wholesaler such as Ingram Books, which fills orders to most booksellers. For pBooks, it's worth it to pay an extra fee for an ISBN assigned to your name, not the printer's name.

For a comparison of the costs of many of the most popular author-services programs, see this article:

http://selfpublishingnews.wordpress.com/2008/03/05/self-publishing-companies-cost-comparison-and-quality-comparison

Strike with Lightning

You can probably earn more money with your pBook by working directly with Lightning Source Inc., one of the industry's largest POD printers. The big advantage of Lightning Source is that it makes your book available through Ingram, the largest U.S. book wholesaler. Whenever Amazon or another retailer orders your book, copies are printed and available within 24 hours. Lightning Source pays publishers once a month, about 90 days after the sales period.

Here is one example of why working with Lightning Source can be more profitable. As mentioned in the introduction to this book, my title *eBay 101* sold 3,192 paperback copies during 2008. After expenses, my profit on each copy was $10.88, so I earned $34,734.63 for the year.

If I had used an author-service company, however, I would have paid more for printing, and had less control over pricing and discounts. For example, one of the most economical firms is Amazon's CreateSpace, which offers a book price calculator here:

www.createspace.com/Products/Book

Using CreateSpace's "Pro" program, the royalty per book came to $7.52. That's a difference of $3.36 per book, which adds up quickly:

	Lightning	**CreateSpace**
Retail price	$18.95	$18.95
Royalty	$10.88	$7.52
Annual profit	$34,734	$24,049
Difference	+$10,685	

As you can see, I earned close to $11,000 more using Lightning Source. The reason is that CreateSpace keeps 40 percent of each sale, while I only gave Lightning 20 percent (known as a "short discount.)

Working directly with Lightning Source is more complicated than simply uploading your files to an author service like CreateSpace or Lulu. To go this route, you've got to be proficient with desktop publishing, or find someone who can help you. An excellent guide to working with Lightning Source is *Aiming at Amazon* by Aaron Shepard.

Lightning Source charges setup fees totaling about $75 for each title, and an annual distribution fee of $12. By contrast, some author-service firms charge no setup fees but, as stated previously, you'll pay more in the long run if your book sells more than a few copies.

Certainly there are cases where an author-service firm like CreateSpace is the smartest route—especially if you only need a few dozen copies of your book and don't expect to publish another title. Authors who don't want to risk the Lightning Source setup fees sometimes go with an author-service company for their first book. If the book sells well, they sometimes switch printers.

If you're publishing your first paperback, one way to get started is to hire a "book shepherd" to navigate the steps of publishing. To locate a book shepherd, consult the "More Resources" section in the back of this book.

The major alternative to Lightning is Replica Books, which is part of a major U.S. book wholesaler, Baker & Taylor. For more information, see Republicabooks.com.

If your book sells many thousands of books annually, POD might not be the best choice. Offset printing, which uses metal plates on a traditional printing press, can drastically reduce your per-book cost when you're printing at least a few thousand copies. The disadvantage for self-publishers is you need cash to pay the printer. Shipping and warehousing costs money, too.

To determine your costs for high-volume, offset printing, use the calculator here:

http://www.rjcom.com/printing

You might find a better price with a printer listed in your local Yellow Pages. Again, it pays to shop around.

Ignore bookstores

Unless and until you and your book are nationally known, you should focus on selling to online customers. The advice in this book is about playing the percentages. Selling your book to bookstores introduces significant risks and upfront investment to the equation. One exception would be if your book has strong regional interest, in which case you have a chance of persuading local stores to stock and display your book.

Getting into bookstores is a losing battle for most self-publishers—even if you win, you lose. The big chains don't want to deal with individual publishers, and are reluctant to carry self-published books even when available through a national wholesaler. Using the short-discount Print on Demand business model advocated in this book also makes it very unlikely that stores will carry your book.

Bookstores are lousy places to sell books.

—Dan Poynter, author, *The Self Publishing Manual*

Perhaps you will sell fewer copies of your book, but you'll have a better profit margin and much less risk by focusing on online buyers. In any case, if your book is available through a major wholesaler, bookstores can place a special order when customers ask for your book.

Designing your pBook

The interior design of your pBook is a technical task you'll need to master or outsource to an experienced professional. This concerns the style of your typography, headers and footers, page numbering, paragraphs, and so forth. If you are composing your book using the OpenOffice Writer word-processing software mentioned previously, you can select from several book templates posted here:

http://www.lulu.com/en/help/templates

For an excellent tutorial on book design using Writer, read *Design a Book with OpenOffice.org Writer* by Luke Muehlhauser.

If you're using Microsoft Word and want to learn to design your own book, check out *Perfect Pages* by Aaron Shepard. And several free book templates are offered at Microsoft's Web site:

http://office.microsoft.com/en-us/templates/CT101445101033.aspx

Follow the rules

When it comes to pBooks, there are several conventions worth learning. For example, if your book isn't presented with accurate bibliographic data and standard identifiers, many retailers and libraries won't find it or buy it.

ISBNs. The book industry uses ISBNs, a unique series of 13 digits, to identify books. Think of it as your book's Social Security Number. Usually a new ISBN is assigned to each edition and format of a book, such as large-print and audio editions. Each country has an agency or company that administers ISBNs, and in the United States, it's Bowker Inc. You can purchase a block of 10 ISBNs for $275 at its Web site:

www.isbn.org

Bowker also sells single ISBNs for $125:

http://www.myidentifiers.com/index.php?ci_id=1567&la_id=1

Although they are relatively expensive, ISBNs are essential to the print book trade. Your ISBN must appear on your pBook's copyright page and near the bottom of the back cover, along with a barcode representing the ISBN and the list price. The ISBN agency will provide the barcodes for an extra fee, or you can generate barcodes at no cost at this Web site:

www.tux.org/~milgram/bookland

If you're working with a cover designer or an author-services company such as CreateSpace or Lulu, you can ask to have the cover design, barcode and ISBN included in your bundle of services. But if your aim is to save money and maximize your profits and control over the long term, you should buy a block of ISBNs directly from Bowker. You'll get a discount by buying a block of ISBNs, and you'll ensure that you are the publisher of record, not some other company.

Once your pBook is finished and you've assigned the ISBN, you can add your title and bibliographic information to "Books in Print," an industry directory maintained by Bowker. This will expose your book to wholesalers, distributors, retail chains, independent retailers, online retailers, schools, libraries, and universities. See:

www.bowkerlink.com

Design your book cover

If you're using Amazon's CreateSpace to publish your paperback, you can use the service's free cover generator. After uploading your text, click the link for "Create a Cover." If you want a more customized cover, download a cover template from CreateSpace, which Amazon will size to match the dimensions of your book. To finish the cover using a graphics-design program such as Adobe PhotoShop, OpenOffice Draw, or Microsoft Digital Image Pro, consult this free guide by author April Hamilton:

http://www.aprillhamilton.com/resources/CreateSpaceBookCover.pdf

If you're not familiar with any of the graphics-design programs mentioned above, it's possible to create a cover using Microsoft Word. Consult this guide by publisher Morris Rosenthal:

http://www.fonerbooks.com/print.htm

You might find a suitable photograph or artwork to use in your cover by searching one of several "royalty-free" stock photo libraries. Licensing fees vary from a few dollars to several hundred dollars. You may be required to credit the photographer by name, so check the terms of the agreement printed on the Web site. Two sites with a wide variety of professional, inexpensive photos are:

http://www.bigstockphoto.com

http://www.dreamstime.com

For more details on Amazon's product image requirements, see:

http://www.amazon.com/gp/help/customer/display.html?
ie=UTF8&nodeId=200109520

If you'd rather find an experienced freelancer to design your cover, consult the "More Resources" section of this book.

Fulfill pBook orders

If your pBook is being printed by Lightning Source or an author-services company is providing your distribution, you don't need to deal directly with customers unless you want to. Retailers will be able to order your book directly from the wholesaler. But you may want to sell some copies, including autographed copies or slightly damaged books, directly.

With some self-publishers, pBooks are a sideline for another business, such as consulting or professional speaking. In this case, it can be worth the extra trouble to fulfill orders yourself because once you have the name and address of buyers, you have the opportunity to offer additional products and services. By contrast, if Amazon or another retailer is shipping the book to the customer, you won't receive the customer's name, address, or e-mail. Some publishers use a hybrid sales model, or a combination of direct sales and other sales mechanisms.

Evaluate Amazon Advantage

Amazon's Advantage program is the company's inventory consignment program for small and mid-size publishers of books, and music and videos published as CDs or DVDs. With Advantage, publishers ship their items to Amazon's warehouse at their expense. Amazon sells the merchandise on its site and handles all the customer service and shipping.

Amazon Advantage has some serious disadvantages if you're using the POD business model described in this book. Most importantly, Advantage requires a wholesale discount of 55 percent. For example, if your title's suggested retail price is $20, your wholesale price is $9—that's how much money you'll net on each sale. So that $9 is all you have left to cover printing and shipping each book to Amazon's warehouse.

You can apply online for the Advantage Program and submit your titles for consideration. If approved, you'll list your items in Amazon's catalog, provide descriptive content, and ship books to an Amazon warehouse. When a customer purchases your title, Amazon processes the order within 24 hours. Amazon tracks your inventory and sends e-mail requests for you to ship more copies to their warehouse based on customer demand. For your previous month's sales, Amazon deposits money into your checking account via electronic funds transfer.

To apply for Advantage, visit this page:

http://advantage/gp/vendor/public/join

It's important to remember that Advantage is a consignment sales model; you're not earning money when you ship your titles to Amazon. Payments are made for sold units at the end of the following month. In other words, if a copy sells during March, you'll get paid by Amazon on the last day of April.

Manage your Advantage account

As an Advantage member, you'll be able to manage the detail page content for all your titles. You'll be able to upload bibliographic data, descriptions, editorial reviews, and artwork.

Advantage also provides online sales and inventory reports. The reports, updated daily, show:

- Unit sales last month.
- Unit sales this month.
- Current inventory.
- Status of the last order that Amazon.com placed with you to replenish your inventory.
- Amount of your next payment.

Advantage Professional. Amazon offers different terms for publishers of certain high-priced, specialized books.

Advantage Professional is nearly identical to the regular Advantage program except that it offers more flexibility on discount rates. To be eligible for the program, publishers must enroll five or more qualified titles that sell for at least $35 per unit. Self-help and How-to titles aren't considered for Advantage Professional.

The Advantage Professional program is often suitable for:

- Publishers of higher-priced professional, technical, and medical books.
- Providers of educational DVDs, videos, or CDs that are scholarly, professional, or technical in nature, and not widely available through normal retail channels.
- Non-profit (501(c)3) groups.

To enroll in Advantage Professional, complete the survey here:

http://advantage.amazon.com/gp/vendor/public/professional

Each book title must have a valid ISBN. Video and music products must have an ISBN or an EAN printed on the back of each copy, along with a corresponding barcode. If the product is shrink-wrapped or otherwise encased, the barcode must be scannable from the other package. Non-scannable items may incur an extra handling fee or be returned at your cost.

Sell on Amazon Marketplace

If you want to sell some pBooks directly to readers and don't mind dealing with individual buyers, a handy sales channel is Amazon Marketplace. This part of Amazon enables virtually anyone, small publishers, bookstores, or individuals, to sell new and used items on Amazon. Amazon collects the payment from your buyer and deposits the funds to your bank account, so there's no need for PayPal, checks or other payment mechanisms. Sellers receive a shipping credit to offset the costs of packaging and shipping.

Sellers pay Amazon a 15 percent commission on each Marketplace sale, plus a $1.23 transaction fee and 99-cent "closing fee."

If you already have an Amazon consumer account, you can use that account to list items for sale. From the item's product page, click the link "Sell Yours Here." Amazon's Web site will prompt you for additional information, such as the bank account number where the proceeds will be deposited. Buyers who purchase using Amazon Payments receive money-back guarantee coverage up to $2,500 under a program known as Amazon's A-to-Z Guarantee.

It's also possible for booksellers to accept Amazon payments on their own Web site. Participating merchants can use a familiar Amazon "Pay Now" button by using a a bit of code supplied by Amazon. For more information:

https://payments.amazon.com/sdui

Fulfillment by Amazon

If you want to sell pBooks on Amazon Marketplace but don't want the chore of shipping to individual customers, you can use the Fulfillment by Amazon (FBA) program to outsource all the customer support functions to Amazon. Participating sellers ship inventory to one of several warehouses.

Like Amazon Advantage, FBA is an option for booksellers who want to sell existing or slightly damaged books already in inventory. Sellers pay a variety of miscellaneous fees for warehousing and shipping your items, in addition to the regular Marketplace commission of 15 percent. The costs of FBA depend on the size and weight of the inventory you send to Amazon's warehouse.

FBA is also available for merchandise sold outside Amazon's site. With this option, which Amazon calls "Basic Fulfillment," you could offer pBooks for sale on your Web site, eBay, or elsewhere, and have those orders handled via FBA.

For complete information about FBA and its fees, consult this section of Amazon's Web site:

http://fba.amazon.com

Write off your expenses

If you're a self-employed writer who earns income from publishing, then by default you're a one-person publishing company. You simply report that income on your tax return, and pay the required taxes.

On the positive side, once you're operating a publishing company, some of the money you're spending on publishing is deductible on your tax return. For example: Books you consult to operate your business, certain travel expenses, and the portion of your home, Internet service, and utilities used for your business.

If you're a one-person company publishing through a service like Lightning Source or Amazon's CreateSpace, you'll receive a Form 1099 listing your taxable income, and you'll list the 1099, plus any other income, on your tax return.

When you're running a business, you need good records to prepare your tax returns competently. You must document the income, expenses, and credits you report on your return. Business records must be available in case the Internal Revenue Service demands an inspection at any time. If the IRS asks for an explanation of your tax returns, complete records will help conclude the examination quickly.

In addition to staying on the right side of the law, keeping good business records will help you manage your business more effectively through these critical tasks:

- **Monitoring your business's progress.** Records will show whether your business is improving or faltering, where sales are coming from, and what changes in your practices might be appropriate. Good records give you a better chance of making your business succeed.

- **Preparing financial statements.** Good records are essential for preparing accurate financial statements. These statements can aid in any necessary dealings with your bank and creditors, as well as help you make business decisions.
- **Identifying receipt sources.** Your business will have money and goods coming in from various sources, and you'll need to keep this information separate from personal receipts and other income.

Your legal structure

If you decide to pursue publishing as a regular endeavor, you'll need to decide how your business will be formally organized and how you'll meet your tax obligations. As your business grows, you should periodically revisit the question of the best form of organization for your business.

Sole proprietorship. Establishing a sole proprietorship is cheap and relatively simple. This term designates an unincorporated business that is owned by one individual, the simplest form of business organization to start and maintain. You are the sole owner and you take on all the business's liabilities and risks. You state the income and expenses of the business on your own tax return.

Any business that hasn't incorporated is automatically a sole proprietorship. So if you haven't incorporated, formed a partnership, or established a limited liability company, your business is a sole proprietorship by default.

The good news about a sole proprietorship is that you're entitled to all the profits from the business. On the other hand, you are 100 percent responsible for all debts and liabilities. So if your business is sued, your personal assets could be seized.

As a sole proprietorship, you're liable for paying income tax and self-employment tax (Social Security and Medicare taxes), and for filing quarterly estimated taxes based on your net income. Since you don't have an employer reporting your income and withholding a portion of your paycheck for taxes, you must inform the

IRS about your publishing income and make quarterly tax payments on the profits. Quarterly installments of the estimated tax, submitted with Form 1040-ES, are due April 15, June 15, September 15, and January 15 of the following calendar year. If you don't yet sell full-time and you also work at a job where your employer withholds income for taxes, you can ask your employer to increase your withholding. That way you might avoid having to mail in quarterly estimated payments on your profits.

As far as the IRS is concerned, a sole proprietorship and its owner are treated as a single entity. Business income and losses are reported with your personal tax return on Form 1040, Schedule C, "Profit or Loss From Business."

If you've never filed a Schedule C with the IRS before, you might wish to hire an accountant to assist you with the first year's return. The following year you might complete the return yourself. One helpful tool in this regard is tax-preparation software such as TurboTax or TaxCut. Unlike the IRS instruction pamphlets, these products guide you through the tax-filing process in plain English. The program can save you several hours at tax time because you don't have to decipher the arcane language of the IRS.

Partnership. A partnership is the relationship between two or more persons who agree to operate a business. Each person contributes something toward the business and has a stake in its profits and losses. Partnerships must file an annual information return to report the income and deductions from operations. Instead of paying income tax, the partnership "passes through" profits or losses to the partners, and each partner includes their share of the income or loss on their tax return.

Corporation. In a corporation, prospective shareholders exchange money or property for the corporation's stock. The corporation generally takes deductions similar to those of a sole proprietorship to calculate income and taxes. Corporations may also take special deductions.

Limited liability company. A limited liability company (LLC) is a relatively new business structure allowed by state statute. LLCs are popular because owners have limited personal liability for the company's debts and actions, as is also the case for a corporation.

Local ordinances

Ask your county government's headquarters to see if any permits or licenses are required for your publishing business. Some cities, counties, and states require any business to get a business license. If you're working at home, your city or county may require a "home occupation permit" or a zoning variance, and you might have to certify that you won't have walk-in retail customers. Since your business is likely an online and mail-order business, this shouldn't be a problem.

If you are conducting your business under a trade name or a nickname, you should file a "fictitious name" certificate with your county or state government office so people who deal with your business can find out who the legal owner is. This is also known as a DBA name (Doing Business As) or an "assumed name."

Sales taxes. Although the Internet is a "tax-free zone" in many respects, this does not apply to state sales taxes for goods sold to customers in your state. To pay the tax, you'll need to open an account and obtain a "resale license," known as a resale number or sales tax certificate in some instances.

You don't collect state sales tax on orders shipped outside your state, however. This is because Internet sales, as well as fax, telephone, and mail-order sales, shipped to another state aren't subject to sales tax unless you have an office or warehouse located there. In some states, shipping and handling fees are not subject to sales tax, but in some they are—you will need to investigate the issue for your home state. This is the way things operate today, but there's no guarantee it will stay this way.

Once you've made the decision that your business is no longer a hobby, obtain a resale certificate from your state tax office. This will relieve you of paying state sales tax on items you buy for resale, but it will also obligate you to report and pay taxes on the sales you make to customers within your state.

A caveat: State sales taxes are an evolving area you'll need to monitor. Because online sales are growing so rapidly, local governments are salivating at the prospect of collecting local sales taxes from retailers, no matter where the item is shipped. Sooner or later, it's inevitable that online sales will be regulated and taxed more than they are today.

If your state requires you to charge sales tax on your shipping and handling charges, you can select the check box labeled "Also charge sales tax on S&H."

Income taxes. Your form of business determines which income tax return form you have to file. For the majority of beginning publishers, a sole proprietorship makes the most sense.

Many beginning sellers spend lots of time dreaming about what they'll be able to "write off" on their tax return, now that they have a business. Actually, what you're doing is paying taxes on your net profits. Your write offs are the costs of doing business, such as buying inventory and paying for postage. What's left over is the profit, and you pay income tax on that.

As far as the IRS is concerned, your business must become profitable within three years or it will be considered a hobby, and none of the expenses will be deductible. For example, your mileage to conduct research for your book is deductible for tax purposes. But don't rely on your memory to keep track of such expenses. Keep a notebook in your car to document the mileage and expenses for your business trips. If you're ever audited, the IRS will want to see documentation for your travel and other deducted expenses.

To figure your taxes, you'll need to keep track of every penny involving your business. Keep receipts and records, and put your expenses into categories such as "postage," "shipping supplies," "inventory," and so on.

Your bookkeeping chores can be greatly simplified with financial software such as Quicken. Most banks offer free downloads of your transactions, and once you set it up, Quicken can automatically categorize all your business expenses and eliminate most of the headaches at tax time. If you have a debit or check card linked to your account, you can use the card for nearly all your business transactions. Those records can be downloaded into Quicken right along with your banking records, making your bookkeeping that much simpler.

If you're familiar with bookkeeping and accounting principles, you might be able to do a better job with QuickBooks software, which is designed especially for small-business accounting.

Supporting documents. The law doesn't require any particular record-keeping technique, as long as you can plainly show your income and expenses. Your records must summarize your business transactions, showing your gross income, deductions, and credits. It's a good idea to have a separate checking account for your business so that your personal funds are not included.

You should preserve the paper trail of any purchases, sales, and other transactions, including any invoices or receipts, sales slips, bills, deposit slips, and records of canceled checks. Keep documents that support your tax return organized and in a secure place. More detailed information is available in IRS Publication 583, "Starting a Business and Keeping Records."

Business use of your home

You may be able to deduct expenses related to the business use of parts of your home. This deduction is subject to certain requirements and doesn't include expenses such as mortgage interest and real estate taxes.

To qualify to claim expenses for business use of your home, you must use part of your home exclusively and regularly as your principal place of business or for storage. This means the area used for your business must be a room or other separate identifiable space, but you are not required to designate the space by a permanent wall or partition.

There are some exceptions to the "exclusive use" test. If you use part of your home to store inventory, you can claim expenses for the business use of your home without meeting the exclusive use test, but you must meet these criteria:

- Your business is selling wholesale or retail products.
- You keep the inventory in your home for use in your business.
- Your home is your business's only fixed location.
- You use the storage space on a regular basis.
- The space used for storage is a separately identifiable space suitable for storage.

To qualify under the regular use test, you must use a specific area of your home for business on a regular basis. "Incidental" or "occasional" business use is not regular use as far as the IRS is concerned.

Insurance. Home-based businesses aren't usually covered under a regular homeowners or renter's insurance policy. So if you have an inventory of physical books, a loss of those items is probably not covered. Likewise, if a delivery person is injured at your home, you may be liable unless an "endorsement" or "rider" is added to your homeowner's or renter's insurance policy. The cost of the additional premium is usually quite low for a business without employees or a huge inventory, so it's well worth considering.

Bookkeeping. For a small publishing business, simple "cash basis" bookkeeping should suffice. The cash method entails recording income when money is received and expenses as they are paid. "Cash basis" does not necessarily mean your transactions are in cash, but refers to checks, money orders, and electronic payments as well as currency. If you're not familiar with the basics of bookkeeping, read *Small Time Operator: How to Start Your Own Business, Keep Your Books, Pay Your Taxes and Stay Out of Trouble* by Bernard Kamoroff.

Cash accounting is simpler to understand and use than the other type of bookkeeping, accrual accounting. Businesses are allowed to use cash accounting if annual sales are below $1 million.

Hiring employees. The decision to begin hiring employees is a big step for any business. Although employees can enable you to expand your selling and profits, hiring will add tremendously to your paperwork and the extent to which your business is regulated by the government. Having employees means that you need to keep payroll records and withhold income, Social Security, and state taxes, as well as Medicare and worker's compensation insurance. The states and the IRS require timely payroll tax returns and strict observance of employment laws. Penalties are usually swift and severe for failure to pay payroll taxes.

Don't be tempted to pay cash "under the table" for help instead of actually hiring employees during their transition from a one-person shop to employer status. There is no gray area here— such practices are illegal because payroll taxes and worker's compensation insurance aren't being paid.

An alternative to taking on employees is to hire independent outside contractors. You can hire contractors as needed, and the practice entails less paperwork and none of the headaches of paying employment taxes or producing payroll tax returns.

If you hire an independent contractor, make certain the person doing the work understands completely that he or she is not an employee. Numerous small-business owners have gotten into scrapes with state and federal regulators when their independent contractors were later denied unemployment compensation or were found not to have paid their own Social Security taxes.

Getting advice. The U.S. Small Business Administration offers free counseling and workshops. The free answer desk is (800) 827-5722. Or, look up your local SBA office in the phone book. The agency's Web site is:

www.sba.gov

Ask your local SBA office if there is a local chapter of SCORE, the Service Corps of Retired Executives, a network of experienced business operators who can provide free help.

Protect your content

The Internet is a great publicity vehicle because it makes your content available to all. By the same token, the openness of the Web can make it easy for people to steal your work. An unscrupulous blogger or Webmaster can copy and paste your most valuable material onto his site within minutes without asking permission.

Every month or so, you should search the Web for some of the text from several of your pages. A Google search for a string of six to eight words within quotation marks should turn up any sites that have copied your content.

A stern message to the owner of the site—or, failing that, the company that hosts the site—usually results in deletion of the stolen material. Here's an example of a cease-and-desist notice you can send via e-mail:

Dear John Doe,

It's come to my attention that you are republishing my original content from MySite.com on your Web site, YourSite.com. For example, page [ADDRESS] on your site includes the following paragraphs: [TEXT].

Your unauthorized use of my original material violates U.S. and international copyright laws. If the offending material remains available on your site 72 hours from now, I will have no choice but to pursue legal action against you.

Please comply with my request, so that we can remedy this situation without unnecessary difficulty.

Sincerely,
Jane Doe
MySite.com

Register your copyright

Copyright is protection provided by U.S. law to authors of "original works" of writing and other intellectual works. Protection covers published and unpublished works. The Copyright Act gives the copyright owner exclusive rights for, among other things, reproducing the work, and preparing derivative works.

Copyright protection is in force from the moment the work is created. In other words, your writing is copyrighted immediately by the author, except in the cases of "work for hire."

So, no publication or registration at the U.S. Copyright Office is required to secure copyright, although there are important advantages to registration. For example, to file a lawsuit for copyright infringement, you must formally register the work. Also, if you register copyright within three months of publication—or prior to infringement—you can be awarded damages and attorney's fees; otherwise only an award of actual damages and profits is available.

To provide notice of copyright in your work, provide the copyright symbol, the year of publication, and your name. For example:

© 2009 John Smith

To register your copyright with the government, visit:

http://www.copyright.gov/register

The advantages of filing copyright online include:
- A reduced filing fee of $35.
- The fastest available processing time.
- Online status tracking.

More resources

- **Current news on ePublishing:**

www.teleread.org

- **Freelancers**

If you need assistance with marketing, book editing, cover design, or interior design, you can select a qualified freelancer at one of the Web sites listed below. The first site, the Independent Book Publishers' Association, allows you to request bids from editors, designers or printers:

www.ibpa-online.org/vendors/request_bid.aspx

www.ifreelance.com

www.the-efa.org

www.ibpa-online.org/vendors/classifieds.aspx

elance.com

www.ibpa-online.org/pubresources/vend_catlist.aspx

Beware of high-priced marketing programs. It's possible to spend a fortune on book marketing, while failing to generate many sales. Before hiring a marketing firm, ask for a list of references. For tips on using free and low-cost marketing techniques, consult my book *Plug Your Book! Online Marketing for Authors.*

- **More information on formatting and uploading Kindle books at Amazon's Digital Text Platform:**

http://g-ecx.images-amazon.com/images/G/01/digital/otp/help/Amazon_DTP_Quickstart_Guide.pdf

http://kindleformatting.com/faq.php

- **Information on eBook formats through the International Digital Publishing Forum:**

www.idpf.org/

- **Independent discussion groups on self-publishing and print-on-demand:**

http://finance.groups.yahoo.com/group/Self-Publishing

http://finance.groups.yahoo.com/group/pod_publishers

- **Amazon forums on self-publishing paperbacks and other media through CreateSpace:**

https://www.createspace.com/en/community/index.jspa

- **iPhone eBook readers and publishing consulting:**

www.scrollmotion.com

http://www.lexcycle.com

www.AppEngines.com

www.pixelpapyrus.com

- **eBook conversion software:**

http://wiki.mobileread.com/wiki/E-book_conversion

http://calibre.kovidgoyal.net

• eBook management, consulting:

Bookworm provides a platform for readers to manage a centralized library of their e-books, and for publishers to experiment with their ePub-formatted books. The company also provides consulting for eBook publishers:

http://bookworm.threepress.org

• eBook distribution to libraries:

OverDrive provides digital download distribution to Borders.com, eFollett.com, BooksonBoard.com, Waterstone's (UK), Papyless (Japan), hundreds of college bookstores, and other online retailers.

www.overdrive.com

• PDF conversion utilities:

https://createpdf.adobe.com/

http://sourceforge.net/projects/pdfcreator/

http://www.cutepdf.com

• eBook unit owned by Barnes & Noble:

http://www.ereader.com

• eBook unit owned by Canada's Indigo Books:

www.shortcovers.com

Index

Printed in the United States
218220BV00004B/17/P